HOT Springs
& Hot Pools
of the Northwest

HOT Springs & Hot Pools of the Northwest

Jayson Loam's Original Guide

Marjorie Gersh-Young

AQUA THERMAL ACCESS

Hot Springs and Hot Pools of the Northwest:
Jayson Loam's' Original Guide

Copyright 1999 by Marjorie Gersh-Young

Front Cover - Three Forks, OR / Chris Andrews
Back Cover - / West Pass, ID / Bob Seal

Design, layout and production
by Marjorie Gersh-Young

ISBN 1-890880-00-0

Manufactured in the United States

Published by: **Aqua Thermal Access**
              55 Azalea Lane
              Santa Cruz, CA 95060
              831 426-2956
              e-mail: hsprings@ix.netcom.com
              web page: www.hotpools.com

Grateful acknowledgements to:
All of the regional contributors who always went above and beyond their assignment to make this book interesting and accurate. Bill Gumbiner for his careful text editing. Staff members at state parks, national forests, national parks, and hot springs resorts for their cooperation and encouragement. All of you who have written in with updates and information and sent in pictures of your favorite places. Henry Young (my husband) for acting both as my sounding board and making the computer run right, and for his final editing of the manuscript. His "eagle eye" caught many of my mistakes.

To

Jayson Loam,
"King of the Hot Springs,"
who pursued with passion what
he truly loved to do—researching
hot springs and sharing
his knowledge.
He taught me to love it, too.
May you soak in peace.

Alaska
Page 20

HOT Springs & Hot Pools
of the Northwest

CANADA
Page 30

British
Columbia

Alberta

States East
Page 182

AQUA THERMAL ACCESS

Washington
Page 52

Montana
Page 152

Oregon
Page 62

Idaho
Page 86

Wyoming
Page 166

Companion volume to
Hot Springs and Hot Pools of the Southwest

TABLE OF CONTENTS

INTRODUCTION

By Marjorie Gersh-Young

This book was written with the premise that there is nothing more enjoyable than to soak in a hot spring in ideal conditions. To me this means a beautiful pool with water at 104° cascading in over the rocks out in the middle of the forest at the end of a moderate hike. While definitions of the perfect pool may differ, there does seem to be some standard information that everyone wants to know in order to make an informed choice.

Our hot springs research program started with an analysis of the 1,600 springs listed in the NOAA springs list published by the National Oceanic and Atmospheric Administration. Only seven percent of the listed springs were on public land, accessible without charge, and another fifteen percent were private, commercial enterprises open to the public. Nearly one-third of the locations had temperatures below 90°, so we eliminated them as simply not hot enough. The remaining two-thirds required individual investigation, usually involving personal inspection, which reduced the NOAA list to a usable twenty-two percent. The unusable seventy-eight percent were often old resorts that had burned down, seeps too small to get into, functioning as cattle troughs, or on posted, private land, making them not usable by the public (NUBP).

As many of you may know, Jayson Loam was the original creator of these hot spring books almost twenty years ago. At that time he did the initial field work and made many decisions as to what information should be included or excluded. Over the years we have refined the format, but without going into an analysis of the chemicals in the water, have maintained the basic premise that soaking in geothermal water does feel good. We have continued to designate hot water as anything above 90°. (Occasionally I will include a lower temperature because of setting, natural beauty or location.) Hot wells are treated as hot springs.

Photos courtesy of Chico Hot Springs and The Chamber of Commerce, Hot Springs, Montana

The location of rental tubs, which have now become an integral part of many people's lives, are also included. And, as a special service and option for many of our readers, there is now a listing of nudist/naturist resorts and parks in those states where there are springs listed that welcome visitors with advance reservations. One thing we do not do is send people onto private property where they can get arrested or shot.

This edition retains these basic criteria while expanding the descriptions, providing more detailed directions with GPS sightings, and adding a bit of history whenever possible. I feel sure that these additions will add to the pleasure and usefulness of this book.

I'm certainly glad that I didn't have to endure a hot springs in a wool bathing suit as these waitresses and maids had to do in 1918 when working at the Chico hot springs resort. And, I can't imagine why the women in Hot Springs, Montana only chose to soak their feet when visiting the springs during the 1940s. Going "barefoot all over" in the 90s is certainly more enjoyable.

REGIONAL CONTRIBUTORS

CHRIS ANDREWS, who lives and works in Idaho seems to like nothing better than to hop in his truck, often with his lovely wife and daughter, and travel to hot springs all over the west. He takes wonderful photographs and doesn't mind how far he has to hike to find a spring he hasn't visited.

PHIL WILCOX, also known as "the Solar Man," is semi-retired and lives on a remote piece of land in Northern California. He loves to travel, often in search of hot springs and has recently been seen in many areas of the west researching hot springs for the book. When not traveling, he designs, sells, and installs remote home solar power systems. Send $4.00 for a complete catalog to THE SOLAR MAN 20560 Morgan Valley Rd., Lower Lake, CA 95457. GPS: N 38.5354 W 122.3136.

JUSTINE HILL is a travel writer, photographer, and tour director who has traveled extensively and writes about, photographs and leads tours to other cultures, natural wonders, sacred sites and the great outdoors. She lives surrounded by nature in Topanga, California. For information about her stock photo collection, tours, and related services, contact Justine Hill at PO Box 608, Topanga, CA 90290. 310 455-3409.

BOB SEAL, who along with his very photogenic wife Glenna, his family and friends, do all of us hot-spring enthusiasts a favor by continually visiting, investigating, and photographing hot springs in Idaho, where he lives. He considers it the best way to spend a summer. We agree. Thanks.

HUNTING FOR HOT WATER:
Where it Comes From

The cataclysmic folding and faulting of the earth's crust over millions of years, combined with just the right amount of underground water and earth core magma, has produced a hot surface geothermal flow that often continues for centuries.

Volcanic activity dies down. Igneous rocks which have solidified from hot liquids such as magma are formed in pockets deep in the earth below the remains of the volcano. The magma produces heat which is conducted through a layer of solid rock into the porous level where new water, or water which has never before been on the surface, is believed to be formed from the available molecules. Fissures are formed in the solid rock layer above the porous layer and steam and hot water escape producing hot springs, geysers, and fumaroles. A hot spring is considered to be a natural flow of water from the ground at a single point. It is called a seep if it does not have enough flow to create a current. Springs may come up on dry land or in the beds of streams, ponds, and lakes.

ARTESIAN SPRING

Artesian spring water comes from a source that is located at a higher elevation than the springhead. The water travels from this source deep into the ground where it absorbs heat from the surrounding earth. As gravity forces water down from the source, heated water is forced up to the surface through cracks in the earth. The water here has an average temperature of 95° F.

Photo by Justine Hill

Natural geothermal areas lie in the earthquake and volcano belts along the earth's crustal plates. In many areas due to the earth shifting and moving the hot magma has worked its way closer to the earth's surface. Surface water (water from rain, for instance) soaks into the earth through cracks and crevices down to the area where the hot magma again provides the heat source for the water. If there are no fissures or cracks for the water to use to come to the surface, water can be sought by drilling.

Water temperatures vary greatly. When the water is at least fourteen degrees hotter than the average temperature of the air it is considered to be thermal water (or a hot springs). This definition means that there is a very wide range of what is considered thermal water as the air temperature in Iceland is certainly different from that of a California desert. The overall temperature of the water can range up to the boiling point. Geothermal resources in Italy, New Zealand, California and Iceland have been used for a number of years to heat municipal and private buildings, and even whole towns. In Iceland the early Norse carried hot water to their homes through wooden pipes.

Photo courtesy of Thermopolis Chamber of Commerce

This tufa mound found in Thermopolis, Wyoming indicates the presence of hot mineral water. Lime and gypsum separate out from the cooling waters to make this natural formation. The colors on the mound in shades of greens and yellows are due mainly to algae which grow in the warm water.

As the water travels up through varying layers of the earth, it accumulates different properties. These are classified as alkaline, saline, chalybeate (iron), sulfurous, acidulous, and arsencial. At least as far back as the time of the Greeks and the Romans medicinal cures were attributed to the different chemicals and certain springs were alleged to cure certain diseases from venereal diseases to stomach and urinary tract weaknesses. The waters were administered in a combination of drinking it and soaking in it.

Of the thousands of hot springs found in the United States, most are found in the Western mountains.

Wyoming has a very wide range of minerals in its drinking water provided at the park.

THERMOPOLIS
Hot Springs State Park's Big Spring
WATER ANALYSIS

There are at least 27 different minerals in the water; making it very healthful to drink.

(Approximate parts per million)

Silica (SiO_2)	82
Iron (FE)	03
Calcium (Ca)	76
Magnesium (Mg)	76
Sodium (NA)	262
Potassium (K)	49
Bicarbonate (HC_{93})	766
Sulfate (SO_4)	760
Chloride (CI)	328
Fluoride (FI)	3.7
Nitrate (NO_3)	10
Total Dissolved Solids	2373
Hydrogen Sulfide (H_2S)	4.5
Hardness ($CaCo_3$)	1274

New spectographic analysis adds the following elements making at least 27 all told.

Strontium	20
Lithium	2
Barium	2
Aluminum	1
Chromium	trace
Copper	trace
Lead	0.0004
Manganese	0.2
Titanium	60
Zinc	2
Tungsten	0.10
Vanadium	0.10
Thorium	less than 0.6
Boron	0.56

A Bit of History

Long before the "white man" arrived to "discover" hot springs, the Native American believed that the Great Spirit resided in the center of the earth and that "Big Medicine" fountains were a special gift from The Creator. Even during tribal battles over territory or stolen horses, it was customary for the sacred "smoking waters" to be a neutral zone where all could freely be healed. Back then, hot springs belonged to no one, and understandably, we would like to believe that nothing has changed.

The Native American tradition of free access to hot springs was first imitated by the pioneers. However, as soon as mineral water was perceived to have some commercial value, the new settlers' private property laws were invoked at most of the hot spring locations. Histories often include bloody battles with "white men" over hot spring ownership, and there are colorful legends about Indian curses that had dire effects for decades on a whole series of ill-fated owners. After many fierce legal battles, and a few gun battles, some ambitious settlers were able to establish clear legal titles to the properties. Then it was up to the new owners to figure out how to turn their geothermal flow into cash flow.

Photo courtesy of Chico Hot Springs

Since many of the commercial hot springs were located in remote areas, the establishments often offered to pick up their clients at the nearest railroad connection and drive them to the springs. There are still some resorts that offer this service, particularly in winter, and often by snowcat.

Pioneering settlers dismissed as superstition the Native American's spiritual explanation of the healing power of a hot spring. However, those settlers did know from experience that it was beneficial to soak their bodies in mineral water, even if they didn't know why or how it worked. Commercial exploitation began when the owner of a private hot spring started charging admission, ending centuries of free access.

The shift from outdoor soaks to indoor soaks began when proper Victorian customers demanded privacy, which required the erection of canvas enclosures around the bathers in the outdoor springs. Then affluent city dwellers, as they became accustomed to indoor plumbing and modern sanitation, were no longer willing to risk immersion in a muddy-edged, squishy-bottom mineral spring, even if they believed that such bathing would be good for their health. Furthermore, they learned to like their urban comforts too much to trek to an outdoor spring in all kinds of weather. Instead, they wanted a civilized method of "taking the waters," and the great spas of Europe provided just the right model for American railroad tycoons and land barons to follow, and to surpass.

Around the turn of the century, American hot spring resorts fully satisfied the combined demands of Victorian prudery, modern sanitation, and indoor comfort by offering separate men's and women's bathhouses with private individual porcelain tubs, marble shower rooms, and central heating. Scientific mineral analysis of the geothermal water was part of every resort merchandising program, which included flamboyant claims of miraculous cures and glowing testimonials from medical doctors. Their promotion material also featured additional social amenities, such as luxurious suites, sumptuous restaurants, and grand ballrooms.

In recent decades, patronage of these resorts has declined, and many have closed down because the traditional medical claims were outlawed and modern medical plans refuse to reimburse anyone for a mineral water "treatment." A few of the larger resorts have managed to survive by adding new facilities such as golf courses, conference and exhibition spaces, fitness centers, and beauty salons. The smaller hot spring establishments have responded to modern demand by installing larger (six persons or more) communal soaking tubs and family-size soaking pools in private spaces for rent by the hour. Most locations continue to offer men's and women's bathhouse facilities in addition to the new communal pools, but most have discontinued the use of cast iron, one-person bath tubs.

In addition to the privately owned hot spring facilities, there are several dozen locations that are owned and operated by federal, state, county, or city agencies. States, counties, and cities usually staff and operate their own geothermal installations. Locations in US National Forests and National Parks are often operated under contract by privately owned companies. The nature and quality of the mineral water facilities offered at these publicly owned, privately operated hot spring locations varies widely.

Courtesy of The Chamber of Commerce, Hot Springs, Montana

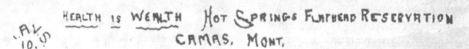

Although natural mineral water (from a spring or well) is required for a truly authentic traditional "therapeutic soak," there is a new generation of dedicated soakers who will not patronize a motel unless it has a hot pool. They know full well that the pool is filled with gas-heated tap water and treated with chlorine, but it is almost as good as the real thing and a lot more convenient. We chose to include in our hunt for hot water those locations that offer private-space hot tubs for rent by the hour.

According to California legend, the historic redwood tub was invented by a Santa Barbara group who often visited Big Caliente Hot Springs. One evening a member of the group wished out loud that they could have their delicious outdoor communal soaks without having to endure the long dusty trips to and from the springs. Another member of the group suggested that a large redwood wine cask might be used as an alternate soaking pool in the city. It was worth a try, and it was a success. Over time, other refugees from the long Big Caliente drive began to build their own group soaking pools from wine casks, and the communal hot tub era was born.

Lehman Hot Springs, "Oregon's Best Kept Secret Since 1871," is located in the Blue Mountains of Eastern Oregon surrounded by 3.9 million acres of forest land.

I don't think *Lava Hot Springs* would mind sharing its spirit with the rest of us.

Photo by Chris Andrews

USING THIS GUIDE

The primary tool in this guide is the KEY MAP, which is provided for each state or geographical subdivision. The KEY MAP INDEX on the outside back cover tells the page number where each of the KEY MAPS can be found. Each KEY MAP includes significant cities and highways, but please note that it is designed to be used with a standard highway map.

Within every KEY MAP, each location has been assigned a number that is printed next to the identifying circle or square. On the pages following the KEY MAP you will find descriptions of each location listed in numerical order.

The Master Alphabetical Index is printed at the end of the book and gives the page number on which each location description will be found. If you know the specific hot spring name, this alphabetical index is the place to start.

The following section describes the quick-read symbols that are used on the KEY MAPS and in the location descriptions.

● Non-Commercial Mineral Water Locations

On the key maps and in each hot spring listing, a solid round dot is used to indicate a non-commercial hot spring, or hot well, where no fee is required and pools are generally created by the rearranging of rocks or by using easily available material. At a few remote locations, you may be asked for a donation to help the work of a non-profit organization that has a contract with the Forest Service to protect and maintain the spring.

The first paragraph of each listing is intended to convey the general appearance, atmosphere, and surroundings of the location, including the altitude, which can greatly affect the weather conditions. The phrase "open all year" does not mean that all roads and trails are kept open regardless of snowfalls or fire seasons. Rather, it means that there are no seasonally closed gates or doors, as at some commercial resorts. Where there is a particular problem we try to note it.

The second paragraph describes the source and temperature of the mineral water and then conveys the manner in which that water is transported or guided to a usable soaking pool. "Volunteer-built pool" usually implies some simple combination of at-hand material such as logs, rocks, and sand. If the situation requires that the pool water temperature be controlled, the method for such control is described. River-edge and creek-edge pools are vulnerable to complete washouts during high runoff months, so often volunteers have to start from scratch every year. Whether bathing suits are optional or not is

indicated. Handicap accessibility is included whenever such information is available.

The third paragraph identifies the facilities and services available on the premises or nearby and states the approximate distance to other facilities and services.

If needed, there is a final paragraph of directions, which should be used in connection with a standard highway map, a National Forest map if applicable, or any local area map. For the many people who now have GPS finders, the coordinates are also included.

Photo by Steve Parsons

Thanks to the many volunteer groups such as those found at Scenic (above) and Bagby (below) without whose hard work these hot springs often would not exist at all, and certainly not in the well-cared for condition they are in.

Photo by Tom Paulu

■ Commercial Mineral Water Locations

On the key maps in this book and in the hot springs listings, a solid square is used to indicate a mineral water commercial location. A phone number and address are provided for the purpose of obtaining rates, additional information, and reservations.

The first paragraph of each listing is intended to convey the size, general appearance, atmosphere, and surroundings of the location. "Open all year" does not imply that the facility is open twenty-four hours of every day, only that it does not have a "closed" season.

The second paragraph of each listing focuses on the water facilities available at the location. It describes the origin and temperature of the mineral water, the means of transporting that water, the quantity, type, and location of tubs and pools, the control of soaking water temperatures, and the chemical treatment used, if any.

In all states, health department standards require a minimum treatment of public pool water with chlorine, bromine, or the equivalent. A few fortunate locations are able to meet these standards by operating their smaller mineral water pools on a continuous flow-through basis, thereby eliminating the need for chemical treatment. Many other locations meet these standards by draining and refilling tubs and pools after each use or after the end of each business day.

There actually are a few commercial locations where rare geothermal conditions (and health department rules) make it possible to soak in a natural sand-bottom hot spring open to the sky.

At those hot springs resorts that are being run as a business, bathing suits are normally required in public spaces. A few locations have a policy of clothing optional in the pools and sometimes everywhere on the grounds. Handicap accessibility is mentioned for those locations that provide it.

The third paragraph of a commercial hot spring listing briefly mentions the principal facilities and services offered, plus approximate distances to other nearby services and if credit cards are accepted. This information is intended to advise you if overnight accommodations, RV hookups, restaurants, health clubs, beauty salons, etc., are available on the premises, but it does not attempt to assign any form of quality rating to those amenities. There is no such thing as a typical hot spring resort and no such thing as typical accommodations at such a resort. Phone and ask questions.

❑ Tubs Using Gas-heated Tap Water or Well Water

Listings of rent-a-tub locations, indicated by a white square, begin with an overall impression of the premises and with the general location, usually within a city area. This is followed by a description of the private spaces, tubs, and pools, water treatment methods, and water temperature policies. Generally, unless stated otherwise, clothing is optional in private spaces and required elsewhere. Facilities and services available on the premises are described. Credit cards accepted, if any, are noted. Nearly all locations require reservations, especially during the busy evening and weekend hours.

In a separate section titled "For the Naturist" we have included a special listing of landed clubs in those states where there are hot springs to give skinny-dippers alternatives to conventional motels/hotels/resorts. Most of the nudist/naturist resorts specifically prohibit bathing suits in their pools and have a policy of clothing optional elsewhere on the grounds. Most nudist/naturist resorts are not open to the public for drop-in visits but the resorts listed in this book are often willing to offer a visitor's pass if you phone ahead and make arrangements.

Photo by Bob Seal

Burgdorf Hot Springs in Idaho is considered a commercial resort because it provides cabins for rent. However, the owners attempt to keep the area as natural as possible. There is no electricity at the springs, so you could consider this cabin-camping.

A Word about Nudity

You had best start with the hard fact that any private property owner, county administration, park superintendent, or forest supervisor has the authority to prohibit "public nudity" in a specific area or in a whole park or forest. Whenever the authorities have to deal with repeated complaints about nude bathers at a specific hot spring, it is likely that the area will be posted with NO NUDITY ALLOWED signs, and you could get a citation without further warning.

The vast majority of natural hot springs on public property are not individually posted, but most jurisdictions have some form of general regulation prohibiting public nudity. However, there have been some recent court cases establishing that a person could not be found guilty of indecent exposure if he removed his clothes only after traveling to a remote area where there was no one to be offended.

In light of these court cases, one of the largest national forests has retained its general "nude bathing prohibited" regulation but modified its enforcement procedure to give a nude person an opportunity to put on a bathing suit before a complaint can be filed or a violation notice issued.

In practical terms, this means that a group at an unposted hot spring can mutually agree to be nude. As soon as anyone else arrives and requests that all present put on bathing suits, those who refuse that request risk a citation. If you are in the nude group, all you need from the newcomers is some tolerance. You may be pleasantly surprised at the number of people who are willing to agree to a policy of clothing-optional if, in a friendly manner, you offer them an opportunity to say "Yes."

NUDITY

Nude bathing is common at Umpqua Hot Springs. If this makes you uncomfortable we recommend you not go into the area.

Please be considerate of others and remain conventionally clothed at the parking lot and on the trail.

A most unusual sign. While much unofficial policy dictates that Rangers not enforce a clothing policy unless there is a registered complaint, it is rare to find a sign that seems to support nudity.

Photo by Chris Andrews

Obviously these soakers at *Umpqua Hot Springs* have come to an understanding where both clothing and clothing-optional can exist side-by-side.

BARE CROSSING

CARING FOR THE OUTDOORS

This is an enthusiastic testimonial and an invitation to join in supporting the work of the US Forest Service, the National Park Service, and the several State Park Services. At all of their offices and ranger stations we have always received prompt, courteous service, even when the staff was busy handling many other daily tasks.

Nearly all usable primitive hot springs are in national forests, and many commercial hot spring resorts are surrounded by a national forest. Even if you will not be camping in one of their excellent campgrounds, we recommend that you obtain official Forest Service maps for all of the areas through which you will be traveling. Maps and information may be obtained from the offices listed below.

Rocky Mountain Region 303 275-5135
Eastern Wyoming, Colorado
740 Simms St., Lakewood, CO 80401

Intermountain Region 406 329-3511
Southern Idaho, Utah, Nevada, and Western Wyoming
324 25th St., Ogden, UT 84401

Nature of the Northwest Region 503 872-2750
Oregon, Washington
800 NE Oregon St. Rm. 177, Portland, OR 97232

Outdoor Information Recreation Center
206 470-4060
Northwest
222 Yale Ave. N., Seattle, WA 98109

Northern Region 406 329-3584
Montana, Northern Idaho
PO Box 7669, Missoula, MT 59807

When you arrive at a national forest, head for the nearest ranger station and let them know what you would like to do in addition to putting your body in hot mineral water. If you plan to stay in a wilderness area overnight, request information about wilderness permits and camping permits. Discuss your understanding of the dangers of water pollution, including giardia (back country dysentery) with the Forest Service staff. They can be good friends as well as competent public servants.

The following material is adapted from a brochure issued by the Forest Service, Southwestern Region, Department of Agriculture and supplemented with up-to-date information by Nancy Pfeiffer.

CAUTION
NATURAL HOT SPRINGS

- Water temperatures vary by site, ranging from warm to very hot . . . 180°F.

- Prolonged immersion may be hazardous to your health and result in hyperthermia (high body temperature).

- Footing around hot springs is often poor. Watch out for broken glass. Don't go barefoot and don't go alone. Please don't litter.

- Elderly persons and those with a history of heart disease, diabetes, high or low blood pressure, or who are pregnant should consult their physician prior to use.

- Never enter hot springs while under the influence of: alcohol, anti-coagulants, antihistamines, vasodilators, hypnotics, narcotics, stimulants, tranquilizers, vasoconstrictors, anti-ulcer or anti-Parkinsonian medicines. Undesirable side effects such as extreme drowsiness may occur.

- Hot springs are naturally occurring phenomena and as such are neither improved nor maintained by the Forest Service.

Please follow signs like this. It seems that every year we lose access to one or two hot springs because people won't stay off private property or close gates when asked.

DO NOT WASH IN STREAMS OR SPRINGS

Wash yourself, your dishes and your clothes in a container, away from water sources.

Pour wash water on the ground away from streams and springs.
If you are near a hot springs, fill a garbage bag with hot water from the springs and wash your clothes in it.

Food scraps, tooth paste, even biodegradable soap will pollute streams and springs. Remember, it's your drinking water, too!

Try to pack out trash left by others. Your good example may catch on!

DON'T SHORT CUT TRAILS.

Trails are designed and maintained to prevent erosion.

Cutting across switchbacks and trampling meadows can create a confusing maze of unsightly trails.

PACK IT IN — PACK IT OUT

Bring trash bags to carry out all trash that cannot be completely burned.

If you see an idyllic green grassy spot to camp right next to the springs, don't use it. Remember, that spot is idyllic to everyone else as well. Also wild animals, bears included enjoy hot springs areas. Give them the right of way. How far away you should camp is up to your good judgement.

CAMPFIRES Use gas stoves when possible to conserve dwindliing supplies of firewood.

Use only fallen timber for firewood. Even standing dead trees are part of the beauty of wilderness, and are important to wildlife.

If you need to build a fire, use an existing campfire site if available.

Clear a circle of all burnable materials.

Dig a shallow pit for the fire.

Keep the sod intact.

If you need to clear a new fire site, select a safe spot away from rock ledges that would be blackened by smoke; away from meadows where it would destroy grass and leave a scar; away from dense brush, trees and duff where it would be a fire hazard. Keep fires small.

Never leave a fire unattended.

Put your fire COLD OUT before leaving, by mixing the coals with dirt & water. Feel it with your hand. If it's cold out, cover the ashes in the pit with dirt, replace the sod, and naturalize the disturbed area. Rockfire rings, if needed or used, should be scattered before leaving.

DON'T BURY TRASH!
Animals dig it up.

BURY HUMAN WASTE

When nature calls, select a suitable spot at least 100 feet from open water, campsites and trails. Dig a hole 4 to 6 inches deep. Try to keep the sod intact.

Don't pick flowers, dig up plants or cut branches from live trees. Leave them for others to see and enjoy.

After use, fill in the hole completely burying waste and taking the toilet tissue with you as animals will dig it up. It can be burned or disposed of later.

ALASKA

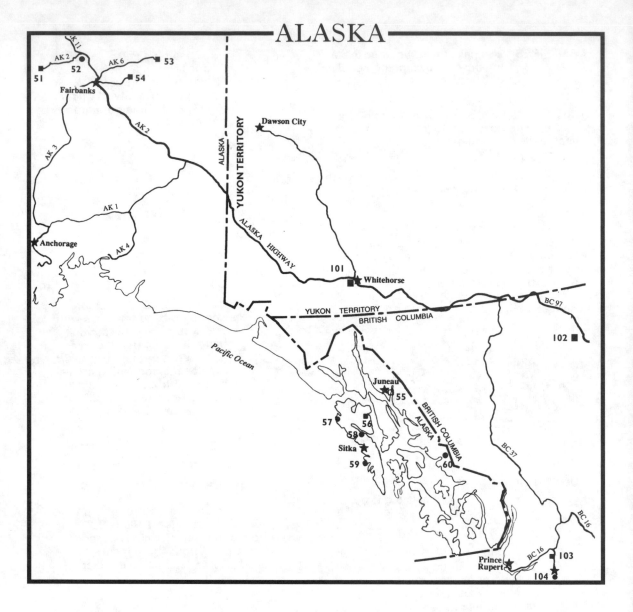

This map was designed to be used with a standard highway map.

MAP SYMBOLS

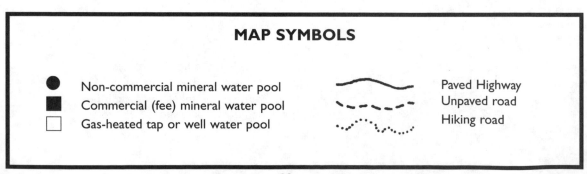

● Non-commercial mineral water pool
■ Commercial (fee) mineral water pool
□ Gas-heated tap or well water pool

Paved Highway
Unpaved road
Hiking road

51 MANLEY HOT SPRINGS
PO Box 50 907 672-3171
■ **Manley Hot Springs, AK 99756**

A unique geothermal greenhouse containing four cement soaking tubs in addition to many flowers and organic vegetables. Elevation 330 feet. Open all year.

Natural mineral water flows out of two springs (125° and 136°) and is piped to the greenhouse for space heating and for use in the soaking pools. Temperatures of 80°, 90°, 95°, and 105° are maintained in the four pools, which are drained, refilled and sanitized each day so no chemical treatment of the water is needed. Tubs are handicap accessible with assistance. Bathing suits optional.

While there are no services on the premises, there are comfortable accommodations at the nearby Manley Roadhouse (907 672-3161), and hunting and fishing are readily available nearby. A 2,700 foot air strip is nearby. No credit cards accepted.

For information, rates, or reservations contact Charles or Gladys Dart at the above number.

Photo by Steve Heerema

Asian pears and bunches of grapes, in addition to baskets of beautiful flowers add to the ambiance.

Courtesy of Manley Hot Springs

52   TOLOVANA HOT SPRINGS, LTD

■   PO Box 83058   907 455-6706
     Fairbanks, AK 99708

Two remote and rustic cabins with outdoor cedar soaking tubs surrounded by spruce, birch and aspen forests, one-hundred road miles north of Fairbanks. Elevation: 800 feet. Open all year; by reservation only.

Natural mineral water flows out of many geothermal springs at 135° and collects in a settling pond that maintains a temperature of 100°. Water from each of these two sources is piped to the two widely separated soaking tubs, allowing complete control of tub water temperature. The apparent local custom is clothing optional.

The two fully outfitted cabins are the only services available on the premises. Bring your own food and sleeping bag. There is a remote air strip two miles from the cabins, and it is eleven miles by all-year trail to the nearest road. It is thirty-five miles to a phone, gas, and an air strip at Minto Village. Local air charters are available. Phone for guided dog sled, snow-machine, or ski trips. Phone for rates, reservations, and weather conditions. No credit cards are accepted.

While a soak surrounded by nature's winter wonderland is magical, it would be wise to heed the words in the Tolovana Hot Springs brochure: "The trails to Tolovana Hot Springs are for the adventurous. Experience is recommended for winter travel." Even in summer it is still an eleven-mile hike, unless, of course, you charter a plane and fly in. Then the hike is only two miles.

Arctic Circle Hot Springs Resort

53 ARCTIC CIRCLE HOT SPRINGS
■ PO Box 30069 907 520-5113
Central, AK 99730

Delightful historic resort hotel and cabins with a large outdoor swimming pool and several private-space pools in the hotel and cabins, 134 miles northeast of Fairbanks. Elevation 900 feet. Open all year.

Natural mineral water flows out of a spring at 139° and is piped to an outdoor Olympic-size swimming pool and to individual hydropools in four cabins, one hydropool in the honeymoon suite and one hydropool on each of the three main floors of the hotel. The swimming pool is maintained at 105°, with a minimum of chlorination. Day use is available at the swimming pool and in the three hotel hydropools. The pools area, deck, and cabins are handicap accessible with some assistance. Bathing suits are required in the swimming pool.

Hotel rooms, cabins, flat space for tents and RVs, a community room for sleeping bags, dining room, saloon, ice-cream parlor (summer), exercise room, massage, and library are available on the premises. Geothermal energy is used to heat all rooms and cabins. All types of hunting and fishing are located nearby and tours can be arranged. A 3,600 foot lighted airstrip is nearby. It is eight miles to all other services in Central. No credit cards are accepted.

Directions: From Fairbanks, drive north on Steese Highway, then east on AK 6 to Central, and east for 8 miles on Hot Springs Road to the resort. Phone for information on rates, reservations, and road conditions.

54   CHENA HOT SPRINGS
■ PO Box 73440   907 452-7867
   Fairbanks, AK 99707

Comfortable lodge with cabins, an indoor swimming pool, a soaking pool, and two whirlpools. Located in a wooded valley fifty-seven miles east of Fairbanks. Elevation 1,200 feet. Open all year.

Natural mineral water flows out of four springs at temperatures up to 156° and is piped to several pools that are treated with chlorine. The glassed-in swimming pool is maintained at 90°; the indoor soaking pool is maintained at 104°; and the two indoor whirlpools are maintained at 100°. The new pool building includes a deck containing an outdoor hydrojet pool that is maintained at 104°. All pools are available for day use as well as for registered guests. Bathing suits are required.

Hotel rooms, cabins, RV hookups (electricity, dump station), laundry, restaurant, and bar are available on the premises. Activities on the grounds include horseback riding, cross-country skiing, snowmobiling, snow cat tours, ice skating, sledding, fishing, badminton, horseshoes, volleyball, gold panning and hiking. It is fifty-seven miles to all other services in Fairbanks. Visa, MasterCard and American Express are accepted.

Directions: From Fairbanks, follow Chena Hot Springs Road (paved) east to the resort. Phone for rates and reservations.

Among the popular activities at Chena Hot Springs, besides soaking in the hot water, are viewing the spectacular Northern Lights and the wildlife that often wanders through the property.

Photos courtesy of Chena Hot Springs

Originally built in 1913, this oldest operating hotel and bar in Juneau has recently been listed in the National Register of Historic Sites and has been refurbished with oak antiques, brass, and stained glass. Hot tubs are for rent in the basement under the name "Juneau Hot Springs."

55   THE ALASKAN HOTEL

167 S. Franklin St.   907 586-1000

Juneau, AK 99801

Hourly hot tub and sauna rentals in an historic downtown Juneau hotel. Elevation 20 feet. Open all year.

Four private-space hot pools, using electrically heated tap water treated with bromine, are available for rent to the public as well as for use by registered hotel guests. Water temperature is maintained at 101°, and each space includes a sauna. The three smaller tubs will hold four persons; the larger one will hold six. Clothing is optional within the private spaces.

Rooms and a bar are available on the premises. All other services are available in the surrounding city of Juneau. Visa, MasterCard, American Express and Discover are accepted.

The hotel is located in the South Franklin Historic District. Phone for rates, reservations, and directions.

56   TENAKEE HOT SPRINGS

■   In the town of Tenakee Springs

A wooden bathhouse containing a concrete soaking pool, built over a hot spring in a tiny, rural Alaskan village with no cars or roads. Elevation is sea level. Open all year.

Natural mineral water flows out of the spring at 108°, directly up into a five-foot by ten-foot concrete container that was built to keep out the sea water at high tide. Men and women are assigned different hours of the day. Bathing suits and soap are prohibited in the pool. Donations are accepted in the adjoining store.

There are no services available on the premises, but rooms, bunkhouse, bar, and laundry are offered nearby in the nostalgic Victorian Tenakee Inn, 800 327-9347. A restaurant and curio shop are located nearby.

The Alaska Marine Highway Ferry stops for only 15 minutes at Tenakee Springs, which is located on the north shore of Tenakee Inlet on Chichagof Island, 45 miles southwest of Juneau.

Tenakee Hot Springs is the main attraction in a town with no cars and single gravel street. The wooden bathhouse has separate hours set aside for men and women throughout the day.

Photo by Katie Corbin

57   WHITE SULPHUR HOT SPRINGS

● **Northwest of the city of Sitka**

Remote hot spring pools with a nearby rentable National Forest Service cabin, within a beautiful wilderness area of the West Chichagof Wilderness Area in the Tongass National Forest, sixty-five miles from Sitka. Elevation 50 feet. Open all year.

Natural mineral water flows out of one spring at 111°, supplying a natural-bottom, outdoor, primitive soaking pool. A three-sided log structure has been built directly over another spring. The pool is in a natural rock depression, approximately four-feet deep. The open side of this shelter, which can be slid open, provides a spectacular view of Pacific Ocean waves crashing on rocky cliffs. Whether to wear a bathing suit or not is determined by the mutual agreement of those present.

There are no services available on the premises, but camping is available on open wilderness land which also provides hiking trails. A forest service cabin behind the bathhouse has firewood, bunks, etc. Access is only by boat, plus a one-mile hike from Mirror Harbor. For cabin reservation information, charter boat rental, and a detailed map to the springs, contact the US Forest Service, 204 Siginaka Way, Sitka, AK 99835. 907 747-6671.

GPS: N 57.807 W 136.341

If it is too cold to sit outside you can get an unrestricted view of the bay and the ocean from the three-sided shelter pictured below. Of added interest are the carvings on the walls of names of past visitors, fishing boats, and items of interest.

Lisianski Inlet Wilderness Lodge and Charters, a family owned concern, offers a variety of trips and charters from something as simple as a hot springs drop-off and pick-up to fully guided Alaskan Safaris. The lodge provides comfortable, spacious rooms, or a private beach cabin with its own kitchen and bath. Meals are included in the price and consist of a variety of traditional Alaskan fare.

They can be contacted at PO Box 765, Pelican, Alaska 99832. 800 962-8441, or leave a message on their machine at 907 735-2266.

Photos above and right courtesy of AnneMarie LaPalme, Sitka Ranger District

58   BARANOF WARM SPRINGS

● **Northeast of the town of Sitka**

Two pools in open-sided gazebos offering views of the the bay and surrounded by the beautiful green trees of the Tongass National Forest. Elevation sea level. Open all year.

Hot mineral water with a faint sulphur smell is piped one-half mile from the source to the two gazebos that are attached to two private dwellings. Please follow the posted directions. The water temperature is approximately 103° in each of the galvanized steel troughs which serve as the tubs. The two tubs together could hold about ten people. Clothing is optional.

A small bed and breakfast and a tiny cafe operate during the summer.

Directions from the boat or floatplane landing: From town follow the boardwalk toward the forest service cabin on Baranof Lake. Halfway between town and the cabin you will see a trail heading south leading toward the springs. You can hear the water and smell the sulphur. During the winter you will definitely encounter snow.

GPS: N 57.085 W 134.839

To get to the springs by floatplane:
  Mountain Aviation, 907 966-2288.
To get to the springs by boat:
  Alaskan Fishing Eagle Boat Charters, Captain Tom Smotherman, 907 747-6759.

59   GODDARD HOT SPRINGS

● **South of the city of Sitka**

Two modern cedar soaking tubs in open shelters overlooking beautiful Hot Springs Bay and located on City of Sitka land on the outer coast of Baranof Island. Elevation 30 feet. Open all year.

Natural mineral water flows out of a spring at 153° and is piped to a double faucet on each of the two tubs. Cold water is also piped to that faucet, permitting complete control of the tub water temperature. There is no charge for using the facilities, which are owned and maintained by the City of Sitka. A primitive "secret tub" is said to be found down a trail into the woods. Whether to wear a bathing suit or not is determined by the mutual agreement of those present.

Boardwalks and stairs have been constructed and camping is permitted in the open spaces, although the usual dampness of the area can make for uncomfortable camping. There are no other services available on the premises. Access is possible only by charter boat or by float plane in good weather. For more information, contact the Sitka Convention and Visitors Bureau, PO Box 1226, Sitka, AK 99835, 907 747-5940.

GPS: N 56.836 W 135.374

Photos by Roger Barnstead

Goddard Hot Springs provides a beautiful view of peaceful Hot Springs Bay. The walkways and stairs put in by the City of Sitka provide access to the tubs.

CHIEF SHAKES HOT SPRINGS

●   **North of the village of Wrangell**

Two large wooden tubs located along the base of a steep, glaciated, granite cliff surrounded by willow and stands of Sitka spruce and hemlock, thirty miles up the Stikine River within the Stikine-LeConte Wilderness of the Tongass National Forest. Elevation 25 feet. Recommended June to October.

Natural mineral water emerges from beneath boulders at the base of a cliff at approximately 120° and is piped to a large wooden tub enclosed in an A-frame structure with insect screening. The other tub is in an open structure overlooking the meadow. A large wooden tub is found up the nearby Kateligh Slough. Whether to wear a bathing suit or not is determined by the mutual agreement of those present. There is considerable traffic evenings and weekends, so please use discretion, and whatever you pack in, pack out.

Changing rooms, a picnic table, fire ring, benches, and outdoor privies are available on the premises. The nearest public recreation cabins (reservations required) are within three miles. All other services are back in Wrangell or Telegraph Creek, BC.

Access is by small, shallow draft boat via Hot Springs Slough, a tributary of Ketili Slough, a side channel of the Stikine River, twenty-eight miles from Wrangell. Ease of access depends on river level; during river levels of less than sixteen feet*, access by watercraft may be limited. It is also possible to fly into Telegraph Creek, BC, and to kayak or motor boat down to the river's mouth. While the rapids are not difficult, there is much submerged material in the river, making it a challenge for beginners. It is recommended that you follow someone down the river the first time; and travel with several spare props and a pole. For cabin reservations, charter flights, boat rental information, and detailed directions to the spring, contact the US Forest Service, Tongass National Forest, Wrangell Ranger District, PO Box 51, Wrangell, AK 99929. 907 874-2323. They also have wonderful maps and printed information.

Source map: USGS *Petersburg C-1* topographic map.
GPS: N 56.717 W 132.005

*The Stikine River level is posted on the internet by the USGS at: http://www-water-ak.usgs.gov/rt-cgi/gen_stn_pg?station=15024800

Information and photos courtesy of David Rak, USDA-FS, Wrangell Ranger District

Dating back to aboriginal times, this site was more recently developed by local citizens for their own use and is currently maintained by the National Forest Service. The trail to the springs begins at the low-water landing and, after a series of log staircases and a log stringer bridge, connects the upper, enclosed tub with the open-air structure below and then continues down to the high-water landing. Along with hot springs enthusiasts, black and brown grizzly bears, moose, wolf, and waterfowl visit the area.

CANADA

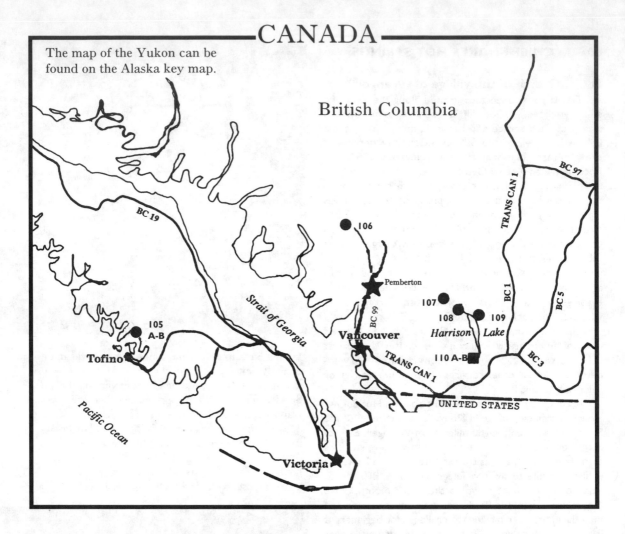

The map of the Yukon can be found on the Alaska key map.

British Columbia

BC 19

BC 97

TRANS CAN 1

● 106

Pemberton

BC 99

BC 1

BC 5

Vancouver

107 ●

108 ●

● 109

Harrison Lake

110 A-B ■

TRANS CAN 1

105 A-B

Tofino

Strait of Georgia

BC 3

UNITED STATES

Pacific Ocean

Victoria

This map was designed to be used with a standard highway map.

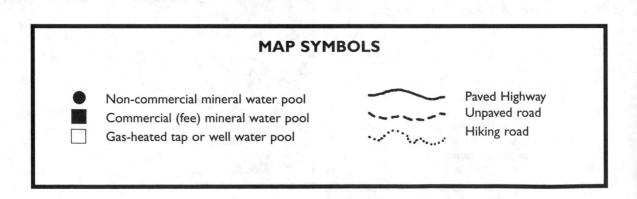

MAP SYMBOLS

● Non-commercial mineral water pool
■ Commercial (fee) mineral water pool
□ Gas-heated tap or well water pool

Paved Highway
Unpaved road
Hiking road

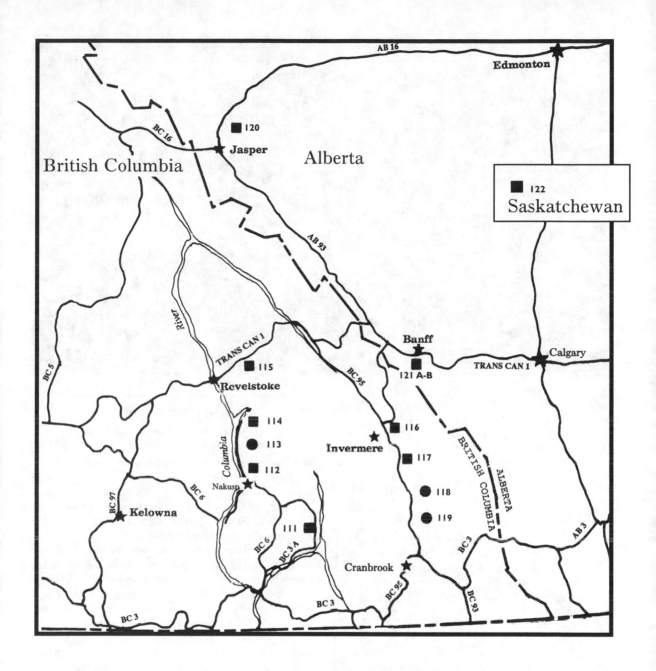

British Columbia

Alberta

Saskatchewan

AB 16

Edmonton

BC 16

■ 120

Jasper

AB 93

■ 122

Banff

Calgary

TRANS CAN 1

BC 95

121 A-B

TRANS CAN 1

BC 5

River

TRANS CAN 1

■ 115

Revelstoke

■ 114

■ 116

● 113

Columbia

■ 117

Invermere

■ 112

Nakusp

● 118

BC 6

● 119

BC 97

Kelowna

BRITISH COLUMBIA

ALBERTA

■ 111

BC 6

BC 3 A

BC 3

AB 3

Cranbrook

BC 95

BC 93

BC 3

Courtesy of Takhini Hot Springs

In the early 1900s trappers gained access to these springs, formed by volcanic action, via the old Dawson Trail or by the Takhini River. During the early 40s, when the Alaska Highway was being built, the US Army maintained greenhouses in the area.

Photo by Phil Wilcox

101   TAKHINI HOT SPRINGS
(shown on the Alaska key map)
RR #2, Site 19, Comp 4   867 633-2706
■ **Whitehorse, Yukon, Y1A 5A5**

Restaurant, campground, and mineral water pool in the scenic Takhini River valley. Daylight lasts from nineteen hours in June to just five and one-half hours in December. Elevation 2,400 feet. Open all year, but closed most weekdays from October 1 to February 28.

Natural mineral water flows out of a volcanic crater reservoir at 118° and is piped to a large outdoor pool, where it is mixed with cold water as needed to maintain a temperature of 102-104°. The pool is drained and refilled each day, so a minimum of chlorination is needed. Some handicap access. Bathing suits are required.

Restaurant, RV and tent campground, sauna, showers, laundromat, and horseback riding are available on the premises. It is seventeen miles to all other services in Whitehorse. Credit cards are accepted.

Directions: Northwest of Whitehorse on the Alaska Highway, turn north on YT 2 toward Dawson City. Drive 3 miles, then watch for the Takhini Hot Springs sign and turn west 6 miles to the springs.

Liard Hot Springs: A beautiful provincial park on the Alaska Highway with a six-foot-wide boardwalk wandering through a wetlands environment where you are likely to view over 250 boreal forest plants—several supported by the hot springs conditions. Wildlife is also prevalent. The Beta pool (above) provides a hot, deep soak and a swim. It was originally developed by the US Army in 1942.

102   LIARD HOT SPRINGS PROVINCIAL PARK
(shown on the Alaska key map)
■ Northwest of Muncho Lake, BC

A lovely, primitive geothermal pond and pool with convenient boardwalk access and a campground, adjoining the Alaska Highway near the Yukon border. Elevation 1,500 feet. Open all year.

Natural mineral water flows out of several springs at temperatures up to 120° directly into a large, shallow, natural pond (named Alpha) created by a low dam across the creek bed. The water cools to comfortable levels as it flows toward the spillway over the dam. Underwater benches are provided for soaking, and the shallow end of the pond is suitable for children. One side of the pond has been improved with stairs, a large deck, changing rooms, and toilets. A six-foot-wide boardwalk has been built through a wetlands environment from the parking area to the pond. Bathing suits are required.

Five minutes beyond Alpha, along a dirt path, is a large natural pool (named Beta) that maintains a temperature of more than 100°. It also has stairs, a small deck, changing rooms, and toilets, but it is used primarily by adults because of the deep water.

There is no charge for day use of the pools, but a fee is charged for sites in the campground. During the popular summer months, campsites fill early in the day. There are no other services available on the premises. There is a cafe across the highway and a lodge within .5 miles. It is 41 miles to all other services. No credit cards accepted.

The park is located at mile marker 497 (765 km) on the Alaska Highway (BC 97) just below the Yukon Territory border. Follow the signs prominently displayed along the highway

The dam pictured on the left creates the shallow Alpha pond that is ideal for children and soakers. Underwater benches are comfortable, and waterfalls are unique.

Photos by Phil Wilcox

103 MOUNT LAYTON HOT SPRINGS
RESORT (shown on the Alaska key map)
■ PO Box 550   250 798-2214
Terrace, BC V8G 4B5

A large, new 1,000-acre destination resort and water park in a beautiful setting on the edge of Lakelse Lake in Western British Columbia. Elevation 800 feet. Open all year.

Natural mineral water flows out of several springs at temperatures up to 186°, is treated with ozone, and is then piped to various pools and waterslides without requiring any other chemical treatment. The outdoor therapeutic pool is maintained at 103° and the outdoor main pool is maintained at 90°. Two of the three big waterslides exit into an indoor catch pool that is maintained at 90°. The third big waterslide exits outdoors into an arm of the main pool. There are also two short outdoor waterslides suitable for small children. Bathing suits are required.

Hotel rooms, dining room and restaurant, bar, and snack room are available on the premises. Fishing and boating are available at adjoining Lakelse Lake. It is 10 miles to all other services in Terrace. Visa, MasterCard, Diners, and American Express are accepted.

Directions: From Terrace, drive 14 miles south on BC 37 to the resort.

Photos by Phil Wilcox

Mount Layton: Three different waterslides can be reached in this tower. Children too small for these big slides have two slides of their own in the shallow end.

Two of the *Mount Layton* waterslides have an indoor catch pool so that fun can continue no matter what the outdoor weather is like.

Just one of the gorgeous vistas as you head up the channel.

Photos by Ron Thiele

104 DOUGLAS CHANNEL HOT SPRINGS

● **(shown on the Alaska key map)**

Eight different natural hot spring sites, some partially improved, along the edges of beautiful Douglas Channel. Accessible only by boat. Elevation sea level. Open all year.

The following three sites are the most popular.

Bishop Bay: One spring, 110°, 15 feet above high tide, supplies a three-foot by three-foot concrete bathhouse. Mooring buoys and a dock are in place.

Weewanie: One spring, 117°, 330 feet above sea level, supplies a small cement bathhouse, built with a grant from Crown Zellerbach.

Shearwater Point: Several springs, 113°, in a fractured rock wall supply a brick pool built by a lumber company for its employees in 1922.

The other sites are difficult to find and/or are flooded at high tide. For more information, contact the Kitimat Chamber of Commerce, PO Box 214, Kitimat, BC V8C 2G7. 250 632-6294, FAX 250 632-4685.

Directions: Kitimat is at the head of Douglas Channel, 36 miles south of Terrace on BC 37.

For those of you who like to sail, this whole area is a sailor's dream, and you can include a hot soak as well.

105A HOT SPRINGS COVE

● **Northwest of the town of Tofino, on Vancouver Island**

Unique confluence of geothermal runoff and ocean waves, located twenty-six nautical miles up the coast from Tofino in Maquinna Regional Park, reachable only by boat or floatplane. The springs offer a spectacular view of the ocean. Elevation 40 feet. Open all year.

Natural mineral water flows out of the main spring at 122°, providing a hot showerbath as it falls over a cliff edge. This geothermal water gradually cools as it flows through a series of soaking pools in a rocky channel leading to the ocean at temperatures of 107-110°. The incoming tide and wave action intermittently splash cold sea water over the visitors in the lower pools. Clothing is optional although the remoteness of this location does not assure you of privacy and it would be a good idea to bring a suit. During summer weekends, you will have plenty of company, which insures a maximum of excitement when the icy waves surge into the tubs. While the walk to the cove is not strenuous there are quite a few stairs which may be a problem for both the elderly and the very young.

You will need to bring a picnic lunch, beverage, bathing suit and towel, good walking shoes, water shoes, sun gear, (light rain gear, if appropriate), a day pack, and your camera. Two restrooms and a changing room are located at the springs. Overnight camping near the springs is prohibited, but a private campground is located adjacent to the fishing boat pier (250 725-3318). Rooms are available in a lodge at a nearby Indian village (250 724-8570).

For information and reservations, contact Jamie's Whaling Station (250 725-3919, 800 667-9913). Based on our experience, they offer a really good trip, which is about six hours round trip. You might want to inquire about whale-watching trips (during certain seasons you are guaranteed a sighting), kayak adventures, and sailing cruises. You'll regret not having a camera.

Photos by Phil Wilcox

The view from the tub on the balcony is magnificent. Treat yourself to the two story room that goes with it.

Hot Springs Cove not only has hot baths in the nooks and crannies between the rocks but lovely, warm water flows over the hillside offering a nice refreshing shower.

105B   **CABLE COVE INN**
       201 Main St.   800 663-6449
       PO Box 339
❑   Tofino V0R 2Z0 British Columbia

Beautifully decorated, romantic inn with a magnificent view of Clayoquot Sound, Meares Island and Wickaninnish Island. Within walking distance of downtown Tofino. A wonderful place to stay before or after a trip to Hot Springs Cove. Elevation sea level. Open all year.

A Continental breakfast is included with the rental of one of the rooms and a shared, stocked kitchen is also available for your use. The "Honeymoon Suite" has a tub large enough for two, and the "Hot Tub Suite" with a second story loft, positions the hot tub out on a large deck with one of the best views of the sound. The remaining four rooms all have tubs with jets, and all rooms offer fireplaces and a view of the ocean. Rooms do not have televisions or telephones. Smoke-free facility. Adult oriented. No pets. One room is handicap accessible. Major credit cards accepted.

Call for additional information and reservations.

● **North of the town of Pemberton**

The largest and most active geothermal area in British Columbia, surrounded by wild rivers, creeks, multiple sources of hot water, and volcanic remains. Elevation 2000 feet. Open all year, road conditions permitting; check in Pemberton.

Water sources ranging from 100-130° (watch where you walk) are carried by sluices to two large wooden tubs where the water temperature in the smaller one cools to 104°. A large wooden tub with submerged benches and a temperature of 110° is furthest from the parking lot. Several rock pools of various sizes and temperatures around 104° are located near various spring outlets and along the creek. Well-built boardwalks and stairs connect all the springs and pools. Clothing optional seems to be the local custom.

Available at the spring are outhouses and picnic tables, tent sites, and overnite parking areas. A small tepee covers a natural hot water source near the creek, serving as a one or two person sauna. The nearest campground and all services are in Pemberton, forty miles south.

Directions: From the town of Pemberton, go north on the Lillooet Forest Road for 14.4 miles, then cross a bridge over the Lillooet River. You will then pass the Coast Mountain Outdoor School. Continue north on the forest road for 24 miles to the junction of Meager Creek and the Lillooet River. Cross the bridge over the river and head southwest for 3.8 miles to a fork in the road. Keep left and continue for 1.4 miles, then cross over the Meager Creek bridge. There is a large parking area located here, as well as a large sign/map showing the various paths to the pools.

GPS: N 50.3425 W 123.2738

Photos by Phil Wilcox

Boardwalks and stairs connect both the wooden tubs and the several rock pools along the creek. Bring a picnic and spend the day trying all the different pools. There may be signs in town indicating the springs are closed. This may not be the case, so inquire.

Photos by Phil Wilcox

107 SKOOKUMCHUCK HOT SPRINGS (LILLOOET) (ST. AGNES WELL)
● South of the town of Pemberton, BC

Three large, fiberglass soaking tubs in a small clearing near a logging road along the Lillooet River. Elevation 250 feet. Open all year; however, the road is not plowed in winter.

Natural mineral water flows out of a spring at 129°. Long pieces of PVC pipe bring a gravity flow of hot mineral water to a large fiberglass tub sheltered by a green steel roofed A-frame. Other pieces of PVC pipe are used to carry a gravity flow from a cold-water spring. Water temperature within each tub is controlled by mixing the hot and cold water. A second tub is out in the open, and the third, large fiberglass tub is shaded by a half A-frame. The use of bathing suits is determined by the consent of those present.

There are toilets and picnic tables available, and numerous nearby self-maintained camping areas along the logging road and at the site itself.

Directions: From the town of Mt. Currie, go approximately 34 miles on a rough logging road along the Lillooet River. At BC Hydro tower #682, turn right onto a camping-area access road and go .25 miles to spring. Caution: This dirt road may require a four-wheel-drive vehicle when wet.

The hot springs are located on private property, and use is permissible without the consent of the property owner. Please respect the hot springs and adjacent property. Pack out all garbage.

GPS: N 49.5758 W 122.2557

Attention all Guests: For over forty years the Trethewey family has held title to St. Agnes Well and the land surrounding it. The hot springs have all been available, at no cost, to any who wish to enjoy these mineral waters. All we have ever asked is that you treat it with the respect the hot springs deserved.

Contrary to what you may have heard or read, there's no government or forestry money spent here. All the improvements you see were provided by E.A. Trethewey.

It is most important that anything packed in is packed the hell out as well, and that goes for those stupid beer cans. If you come into this country with it, you must take it with you when you leave. Believe it or not, it is much easier to dispose of back in the city. Anything you leave behind may habituate a bear to the campsite, which may only die in the end. Please obey the rules on the signs here and in the campground.

Thank you for your time. Robin Trethewey
Anyone care to contribute?
St. Agnes Well, Box 37, Mount Currie V0N 2K0

Photo by Phil Wilcox

108   SLOQUET CREEK HOT SPRINGS

●   **Near the north end of Harrison Lake, BC**

These hot springs are located about sixty-two miles south of Mt. Currie, near the Lillooet River and just northwest of Harrison Lake. Elevation approximately 1000 feet. Open all year, weather permitting.

Water comes out of the springs at temperatures from 135-155°. Several springs seep from the rocks around Sloquet Creek and flow along the ground before dropping over a very hot, short waterfall and forming a small pool that is too hot for bathing. Several other springs percolate from the ground at about 110°, and volunteers have constructed small, natural-rock pools for bathing along the creek. A bucket would be handy to carry cold water to the pools. Clothing optional.

Few services are available in the area, though there is a logging camp at Port Douglas, at the head of Harrison Lake. Walk-in camping is possible near the springs and near the new bridge at the gravel pit, one-quarter mile further on.

Directions: From the town of Mt. Currie, go about 57 miles south on the logging road along the Lillooet River to a bridge that crosses the river to the west side. Turn left, cross Fire Creek, and go south two miles to a second creek, where you go right. Follow this creek (Sloquet) for about 3.4 miles on an old logging road that takes you to a bridge across North Sloquet Creek. A new bridge is being built so that you no longer have to cross the river by foot. Follow the logging road until you reach an obvious clearing that can be used for camping. There is a trail leading downhill from the clearing to the creek and the hot springs. It will take two to three hours to drive from Mt. Currie and an additional 45 minutes to walk the remainder of the logging road to the hot springs. There are no posted rules or regulations for use of the site, but anything packed in should be packed out, particularly garbage.

Directions from Harrison Hot Springs: Head north out of Harrison Hot Springs to 20 Mile Bay Campground which is free and beautiful. Proceed west along the lake for 79 miles, some pretty rough road, to a large logging camp at Port Douglas. Continue 4.2 miles across the Sloquet Creek bridge, turn left uphill, left at the first fork, and left at the second fork to the new bridge. At springs parking area take the left road down hill to springs about .25 miles and very steep. It is an easy 1 hour hike each way. (Depending on weather and road conditions, you can easily drive through, although a 4WD vehicle is recommended for all roads in this area.) It took about 2 hours from Harrison Hot Springs to 20 Mile Bay and another 3 hours from there to Sloquet Creek.

Source map: *Chilliwack Forest District Recreation Map* (springs not shown).

GPS: N 49.4441 W 122.1753

109   CLEAR CREEK HOT SPRINGS
Along the northeast side
●   **of Harrison Lake, BC**

Closed as of 1997 by order of the Forest Service at the request of the "Fisheries Department." According to locals the real reason was too much trash, graffiti, etc.

Courtesy of The Harrison Hotel

110A   THE HARRISON HOTEL

100 Esplanade   **604 521-8888**
                                     800 663-2266

■   **Harrison Hot Springs, BC V0M 1K0**

Attractive, large destination resort located on the south shore of beautiful Lake Harrison, sixty-five miles east of Vancouver. This well-managed facility offers an unusually wide range of recreational activities. Elevation 47 feet. Open all year.

Natural mineral water flows out of a spring at 140° and is piped to cooling tanks before being treated with chlorine. An outdoor swimming pool for adults only is maintained from 95-105°, another outdoor pool for all guests is maintained from 90-95°, an outdoor lap pool at 85°, an indoor pool at 94°, and the indoor soaking pool at 104°. The men's and women's sections of the health pavilion each contain a Roman bath in which the temperature is controllable. Each of the men's and women's dressing rooms has a sauna. Health pavilion services are available to the public, but all other facilities are reserved for registered guests only. One of the outdoor pools is handicap accessible. Bathing suits are required.

A restaurant, bungalows, rooms, children's programs and water park, pickle ball, boat cruises, and boat rentals are available on the premises. All major credit cards are accepted. Phone for rates, reservations, and additional directions.

110B   HARRISON HOT SPRINGS PUBLIC POOL

c/o Harrison Hotel

■   **Harrison Hot Springs, BC V0M 1K0**

Large, modern, indoor communal plunge owned and operated by the hotel, available to the public. Elevation 47 feet. Open all year.

Natural mineral water drawn from the same spring that supplies the hotel is treated with chlorine and maintained at 100°. Pool is four feet deep. Bathing suits are required.

Locker rooms are available on the premises. All other services are within three blocks. Visa and MasterCard are accepted.

Location: On the main intersection at the beach in Harrison Hot Springs.

Photo by Phil Wilcox

Photos by Chris Andrews

111   AINSWORTH HOT SPRINGS
PO Box 1268   604 229-4212
                             800 668-1171
■   **Ainsworth Hot Springs BC V0G 1A0**

Modern, all-year destination resort with a multi-pool plunge and geothermal caves, overlooking beautiful Kootenay Lake. Elevation 1,700 feet. Open all year.

Natural mineral water flows out of five springs at temperatures ranging from 110-117°. The outdoor swimming pool and connected hydrojet pool are maintained at 85-95°. The water in the caves ranges from 104-110° and is circulated to the connected outdoor soaking pool, where it ranges from 104-106°. There is a ledge in the cave that may be used as a steambath. There is also an outdoor cold pool containing creek water ranging from 50-60°. All pools are treated with chlorine. Bathing suits are required.

Facilities include hotel rooms, lounge, dining room, banquet rooms, meeting rooms and dressing rooms. Massage, by appointment, is available on the premises. It is one-half mile to overnight camping and nine miles to a store and service station. MasterCard, Visa and Diners Club are accepted.

Location: On BC 31, 12 miles south of Kaslo and 29 miles north of Nelson.

Nearby camping or a stay in the hotel would make for a wonderful vacation with access to these beautiful pools and a mineral-water cave, something very unusual to tell your friends about when you get home.

Photo by Chris Andrews

A new interpretive trail all the way from the hot springs to the village is a must for all who enjoy hiking in old growth forests.

112 NAKUSP HOT SPRINGS
PO Box 280   250 265-4528
■ **Nakusp, BC V0G 1R0**

One of British Columbia's most modern facilities nestled against the Kuskanax River surrounded by beautiful mountain scenery. Elevation 2,200 feet. Pool open all year (closed for one week late April, early May).

Natural mineral water flows out of springs at 135° and is piped to two outdoor pools where it is treated with chlorine. The swimming pool is maintained at 96° in the summer and the soaking pool at 106°; in the winter the swimming pool is 100° and the the soaking pool 108°. The entire facility is handicap accessible. Bathing suits are required.

Locker rooms, locks, bathing suit and towel rentals, cabins and 38 camping spots along the river (open mid-May to mid-October), cross-country skiing, hiking trails, and creek fishing are available on the premises. A cappuccino and snack bar and a lobby with a view of the pools is provided for your pleasure. It is eight miles to a cafe, store, service station, and RV hookups. Visa and Master-Card accepted.

Directions: From a junction on BC 23 one mile north of Nakusp, follow signs eight miles east to the plunge.

113 HALFWAY HOT SPRINGS
● **Northeast of the town of Nakusp**

Riverside rock-and-sand pools plus wooden tubs located along the Halfway River in a lush, pine forested valley in the Selkirk Mountains. Elevation 2,000 feet.

Natural mineral water at 140° is piped from a spring to two tarp-lined wooden soaking pools approximately seven-feet and four-feet square. A valve located on the pipe is used to control the water temperature. Volunteer-built, rock-and-sand pools are found by the river's edge. Clothing optional.

There are no services on the premises. There is unofficial camping near by and at Box Lake, five miles south of Nakusp. All other services are twenty-three miles back in Nakusp.

Directions: From the Nakusp Information Center in Nakusp (considered mile point 0) head north 16 miles to a logging road on your right (east). 6.4 miles up the road there is a large gravel parking area and a steep trail heading north down towards the river. It is approximately .25 mile down to the tubs and 50 yards further to the pools on the river.

Source map: *Arrow and Kootenay Lake Forest Districts Recreation Map* (springs not listed).
GPS: N 50.50465 W 117.78646

Photo by Chris Andrews

Courtesy of Halcyon Hot Springs

114   HALCYON HOT SPRINGS
PO Box 37   888 689-4699
■ **Nakusp, BC V0G 1R0**

A new destination wellness resort (to open in December, 1998) where everything has to fit into nature and every tub will have a view of Mt. Odin and beautiful, forested surroundings. Elevation 1,900 feet. Open all year for overnight stays; hour and day passes also available.

Natural mineral water at 120° flows out of a hillside and is piped to a variety of pools in a natural post-and-beam design. The hot spring soaking pool, with jets, will be kept at 107°; the warm pool at 95°; and the large kidney-shaped swimming pool at 85°. If any chemicals will need to be added it will be a minimal use of chlorine. Indoor theme rooms and a larger indoor mineral water pool are also available. The whole resort will be handicap accessible. Bathing suits required.

One and two-bedroom chalets, fully furnished, overnight camping cabins, with or without bedding, and holding up to five people, thirty-five camping sites by the lake, and fifty fully serviced RV sites are on the premises. Changing rooms, a small bistro, restaurant, piano bar, gift shop, horseback riding and tours, ATV tours, 250 kilometers of trails, lake sports, and fishing are also being offered. Health services including massage, reflexology, and yoga are also available. Visa and MasterCard accepted.

Call for status of construction, directions, and reservations.

115   CANYON HOT SPRINGS
PO Box 2400   250 837-2420
■ **Revelstoke, BC V0E 2S0**

Well-kept commercial plunge with creekside camping spaces and a spectacular view of the Monashee mountain range. Elevation 3,000 feet. Open May 15 to September 15.

Natural mineral water is piped from Alberet Canon Spring at 85° and is gas-heated, as needed, and treated with chlorine. The outdoor swimming pool is maintained at 85° and the outdoor soaking pool at 105°. Bathing suits are required.

Locker rooms, cafe, store, RV hookups and overnight camping are available on the premises. It is twenty-three miles to a service station and motel in Revelstoke. Visa, MasterCard, and American Express are accepted.

Location: Twenty-three miles east of Revelstoke on Canada 1.

Photos by Chris Andrews

116   RADIUM HOT SPRINGS

PO Box 40   250 347-9485
                          800 767-1611

■   **Radium Hot Springs, BC V0A 1M0**

Home to the Canadian Parks Service largest hot spring pool, with adjacent campground, and surrounded by the beautiful mountain scenery of Kootenay National Park where wildlife abounds. Elevation 2,800 feet. Open all year.

Natural mineral water flows out of several springs that are underneath and along the northeast wall of the hot pool and is collected and redistributed throughout the complex at a combined temperature of 114°. It is piped to two outdoor pools, where it is treated with chlorine. The swimming pool is maintained at a temperature of 82°, and the soaking pool is maintained at a temperature of 104°. A completely refurbished cool pool comes complete with diving board. A new outside spa filled with mineral water is kept cool in the summer and hotter in the winter. The pool complex is fully wheelchair accessible. Bathing suits are required.

Changing rooms (some for families), bathing suit and towel rentals, massage, and a cafe are available on the premises along with a restaurant and a cafe at pool level. The government campground is located on a plateau above the pool complex, and a short trail leads to the pool. Several other campgrounds are nearby, along with a lodge and restaurant. It is one and a-half miles to a store and service station in Radium. The Kootenay National Park Information Center is located in the building. Credit cards are accepted.

117 FAIRMONT HOT SPRINGS RESORT
PO Box 10   **250 345-6311**
■ **Fairmont Hot Springs, BC V0B 1L0**

Famous, large destination resort and communal plunge, located at the headwaters of the mighty Columbia River, beautifully landscaped and surrounded by the forested mountains of the Windermere Valley. Elevation 2,100 feet. Open all year.

Natural mineral water flows out of three springs at temperatures of 108°, 112° and 116° and is piped to the resort pools, where it is treated with chlorine and cooled with creek water as needed. The outdoor public plunge area, also available for day-use, includes a swimming pool, maintained from 87-90°, and a soaking pool maintained at 102°. An indoor soaking pool at 108°, an indoor cold plunge and another outdoor hot pool are reserved for hotel guests only. In addition, an old concrete and rock building on the hillside near the campsites has, what looks like, some of the original soaking tubs built in the early 1900s and still available to day-use customers. Some areas are handicap accessible. Bathing suits are required.

Locker rooms, massage, restaurants, conference center, spa services, store, service station, hotel rooms, full-service RV hookups, saddle horses, tennis, and golf are available on the premises with river rafting, skiing, and other seasonal sports nearby. Major credit cards are accepted.

Location: On BC 93, 64 miles north of Cranbrook and one-hundred miles south of Banff. The resort also has a private airport.

Photos by Chris Andrews

Hotel guests, campers, and day-use visitors have a variety of pools to soak in, including the old bathhouse and outdoor pool (see below) dating back to the early 1900s when the resort was first opened.

Photos by Chris Andrews

118   LUSSIER HOT SPRINGS

● **South of the village of Canal Flats**

A covered staircase leads part of the way down a steep, bare embankment to the pools, which are located on the banks of the Lussier River in the East Kootenays in Southeastern British Columbia. Elevation 3,800 feet. Open all year.

Natural mineral water flows out at 110° into the uppermost wooden pool five by three feet and two feet deep. The second pool with a gravel bottom and rock walls is twelve feet in diameter and about one and one-half feet deep. The third pool is ten feet in diameter and about two feet deep. The water in the third pool can be adjusted by diverting water from a small cold spring into the pool. A good way to cool off is to just step out of the pools and into the river, but watch out for kayackers! The two lowest pools, about eight feet square and one and one-half feet deep, are usually flooded out during all but the driest part of the year (watch for glass in the bottom of these pools). Water temperatures starting at 110° decrease in each pool down the line with the lower pools registering between 100-107°.

There is a small changing room and garbage cans in the parking area and fresh cold water from the river. The nearest campground is approximately three miles east on the same road. A small store is located in Canal Flats, and the nearest gas station and lodgings are to be found in Fairmont, twenty miles north on Hwy 93.

Directions: From the village of Canal Flats, head south on Hwy 93 for three miles to a well-marked turnoff on the east side of the highway to Whiteswan Lake Provincial Park. Follow this road (Whiteswan forestry road) for 11.5 miles. The springs are well marked on the south (right) side of the road (the large sign on the north side indicates the beginning of Whiteswan Lake Provincial Park). As this road is quite busy all year round with logging trucks and mining trucks hauling ore, please drive with your headlights on.

Source map: *Invermere Forest District Map* (BC Forest Service). Phone: 250 342-4200.

GPS: N 50.13575 W 115.57565

Do not turn right (south) here. This is the turnoff to Premier Lake. Turn left (north) on what is now known as Sheep Creek Road. At 5.3 miles, the paved road crosses a river via a sturdy wooden bridge and passes two farms. At 5.8 miles, the paved road ends and is now called White/Ram Forest Road. Turn on your headlights and slowly proceed up this dirt road to mile 13.2. Park your car on the north (left) side of th road. The springs are about 50 yards uphill from where your vehicle is parked. Parking is limited to about four vehicles.

From Skookumchuck go north .6 miles to the turnoff to Premier Lake Provincial Park. Consider this point 0. At .5 miles bear right and continue 4.9 miles to the "T" intersection. (Continue, using directions in above paragraph.)

Source map: *Cranbrook Forest District Recreation Map* (BC Forest Service). Phone: 250 426-1700.

GPS: N 50.03258 W 115.59310

Photos by Rick Slobodian

119   RAM CREEK HOT SPRINGS

● **Between Fairmont and Cranbrook**

Three rock pools located in a ravine halfway up the side of a mountain in the East Kootenays, with a fantastic view and with temperatures perfect for all-day soaking. Also a very good place to view the hummingbirds that frequent the area, but do watch out for spots of poison oak. Elevation 4,800 feet. Open mid-May to mid-November, for those with sturdy cars; any other time can be very dangerous.

Three gravel-bottom, rock-wall pools about two feet deep are each fed by individual springs with temperatures at 96° in the upper pool, 93° in the middle pool, and 88° in the lower pool. The apparent local custom is clothing optional.

There are no facilities on the premises. Drinking water is available from a stream one mile back down the road. The nearest campground is located in Premier Lake Provincial Park, eight and one-half miles back down the road you just came up. The closest gas station is in Skookumchuck one-half mile south of the turnoff from Hwy 93. Lodging and other amenities can be found in Cranbrook, forty-five miles south on Hwy 93, or in Invermere, sixty miles north on Hwy 93.

Directions: From the town of Canal Flats go south on Hwy 93 for 17 miles to a well-marked turnoff to Premier Lake Provincial Park on the (left) east side of the highway. From this turnoff (consider this point 0), proceed east 4.3 miles to a "T" intersection.

Even a difficult drive, limited parking, and an often early snow fall, doesn't discourage people from this often deserted soaking area.

Photos courtesy of Miette Hot Springs

120   MIETTE HOT SPRINGS
Jasper National Park Box 10
403 866-2233
■   **Jasper, AB T0E 1E0**

Dubbed "the hottest hot spot in the Rockies," Miette is located in a remote part of beautiful Jasper National Park with a spectacular view of Ashlar Ridge. Elevation 4,500 feet. Open May to October.

Natural mineral water flows out of several springs at temperatures up to 129° and is piped to two outdoor pools where it is treated with chlorine and maintained at approximately 103°. The first pool is shallow with a lounging area and wheelchair access. The second pool is deeper and has a diving board. A cold plunge was also recently added. The entire facility is designed for handicap accessibility. Bathing suits are required and can be rented, along with towels, at the facility.

Locker rooms are available on the premises. A coffee and snack bar offer picnic lunches and snacks to enjoy at the outdoor picnic area with evening barbeques available. Camping is close by at Pocahontas or accommodations can be had at Miette Bungalows. An interpretive trail leads to the hot springs source and there is much superb hiking area in subalpine mountain terrain with ample opportunity to view wildlife. It is eleven miles to all other services. Major credit cards are accepted and a valid National Park permit is required.

Directions: From the town of Jasper, drive 44 km (26 miles) east on AB 16 to Pocahontas, then turn southeast on Miette Road to the springs.

Jasper Yellowhead Museum & Archives

Miette circa 1935

First developed by the fur traders in the 1800s, a stone and log dam allowed cool water from a nearby creek to mix with the very hot mineral springs water.

121A   UPPER HOT SPRING
Banff National Park Box 900
                                    403 762-1515
■   **Banff, AB T0L 0C0**

Totally renovated and updated this Parks Canada hot springs is surrounded by the beautiful scenery of Banff National Park, 75 miles west of Calgary. Elevation 5,176 feet. Open all year.

Natural mineral water at 117° flows out of a spring located 50 yards southwest of the pool entrance and is piped to a new outdoor swimming with bench seats all around where the water is treated with chlorine. Water temperature in the swimming pool is slightly lower than the current spring output temperature. An enlarged central island includes a children's wading area. Bathing suits are required, and suits and towels may be rented at the pool. All areas are handicap accessible with ramps into the pools.

Changing rooms with heated floors are available on the premises. Also available are family/unit change areas, a spa with aromatic steam, mineral plunge pool, aromatherapy and massage, all available by appointment. On the premises is a licensed restaurant, deck-side snack bar, boutique and gift store. Self-guiding trail explains the natural history of the area. Picnic areas are on the grounds. It is one mile to a store and motel and four miles to overnight camping and RV hookups. Credit cards are accepted, and a valid National Park permit is required.

Directions: From the south end of Banff Avenue, follow signs to the spring.

Courtesy of Banff National Park

121B   CAVE AND BASIN HOT SPRING
Banff National Park
Banff, AB T0L 0C0

The swimming pool was closed in 1992, and only the interpretive center is currently open.

122 MANITOU SPRINGS RESORT HOTEL AND MINERAL SPA

PO Box 967   306 946-2233
      800 667-7672

■ **Manitou Beach, SK S0K 4T0**

Large, new resort hotel and spa featuring indoor pools filled with mineral-rich water pumped from Little Manitou Lake, located seventy miles southeast of Saskatoon. Elevation 500 feet. Open all year.

Lake-bottom mineral springs supply the lake with water three times saltier than the ocean. This highly buoyant water is pumped to three indoor pools, where it is heated with gas and treated with chlorine. The exercise pool is maintained at 94°, the soaking cove is maintained at 98°, and the water massage pool is maintained at 100°. Fully wheelchair accessible. Bathing suits are required.

Hotel rooms, restaurant, bar, gift shop, retail mall, total body care services and massage are available on the premises. A service station and store are located on the corner. Visa and MasterCard are accepted.

Directions: From the town of Watrous, 70 miles southeast of Saskatoon, drive three miles north on SK 365 to Manitou Beach and follow signs to the Spa.

The lake at *Manitou Springs* has a specific density greater than that of the Dead Sea, so it's impossible to sink. What a fun experience!

WASHINGTON

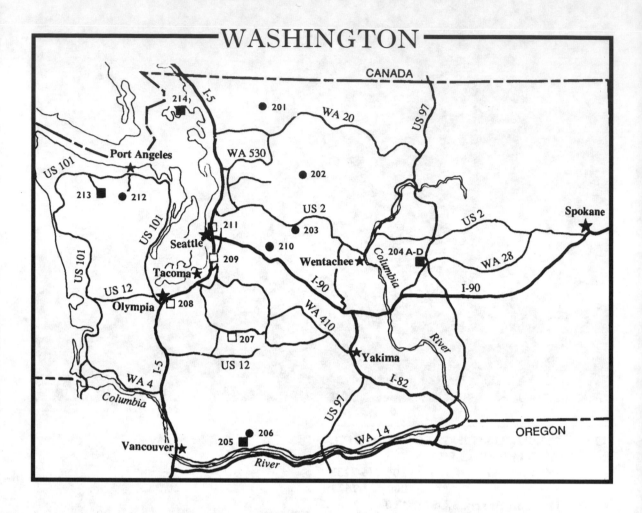

This map was designed to be used with a standard highway map.

MAP SYMBOLS

- ● Non-commercial mineral water pool
- ■ Commercial (fee) mineral water pool
- □ Gas-heated tap or well water pool

~~~ Paved Highway
- - - Unpaved road
⋯⋯ Hiking road

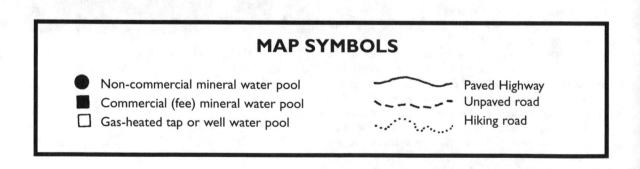

Photo by Phil Wilcox

201   BAKER HOT SPRINGS

● **North of the town of Concrete**

Charming, primitive spring located at the end of an easy 600-yard path through the lush, green timber of Mt. Baker National Forest. Elevation 2,000 feet. Open all year; winter ski-in or snowmobile.

Natural mineral water bubbles up through vents into the bottom of a large, round, sometimes murky, sandy-bottom pool at 95-100°. Water temperature is controlled by diverting the water from a small, adjacent cold stream. Volcanic ash on the bottom of the pools sometimes clogs vents. Dig down to clear the vents and the water temperature is 102-106°. Water spills out through a channel to a nearby shallow "kiddie pool." The apparent local custom is clothing optional, although it is often necessary to be patient when clothed people are using the pool and are uncomfortable with nudity.

There are no facilities on the premises. There is a private resort and campground located three miles away. Facilities include cabins, camping sites with hookups, boating, and a mini-store. It is thirteen miles to a telephone at Lake Tyee Campground. All other services are twenty miles away in Concrete.

Directions: From I-5 at Burlington, five miles north of Mt. Vernon, follow SR 20 approximately 22 miles east to the Baker Lake turnoff. Turn north on Brandy Creek Road for 20 miles to Baker Lake Resort. Directly across from the resort entrance road is a logging road. Follow this unpaved, deeply rutted road for 3.2 miles to a parking turnout on both sides of the road. An unmarked, easy trail begins at the north end of the parking area on your left.

Alternative: From SR 20, follow Baker Lake Road for 18 miles to FR 1130, which is 0.1 miles past the bridge over Boulder Creek. After bridge go .1 mile and turn left onto unmarked gravel road. In 1.5 miles, at fork, go straight toward Rainbow Falls. At the next "Y" turn right on FR 1141 for .5 miles to the parking turnout on left. The trail to the springs will be on the north side. This is a wider, better graded road than the logging road.

Source map: *Mt. Baker-Snoqualmie National Forest* (hot spring not shown).

GPS: N 48.4553 W 121.4013

● **Southeast of the town of Darrington**

A popular hot spring on a long, five-mile, difficult, uphill trail that eventually connects with the Pacific Crest Trail in the Glacier Peak Wilderness. Elevation 3,300 feet. Open all year.

Natural mineral water flows out of a spring at 96°, directly into a four-foot by five-foot cedar-plank soaking box. A deck surrounds the box, and there is a hanging rail for gear. The rusty-colored water bubbles up vigorously into the bottom of the box at 90-92°. There are no posted clothing requirements.

The only facilities are the pit toilet and a source for drinking water near the cabin. There are undeveloped camp sites near the springs and National Forest campgrounds along Mountain Loop Road. All other services are in Darrington.

If you are already hiking the Pacific Crest Trail, then a stop at Kennedy Hot Springs to soak would certainly be welcome. Otherwise, you'll have a very long, difficult hike to get to this pool.

Photos by Justine Hill

Note: Check for possible avalanche or trail wash-outs with the Darrington Ranger Station: 206 436-1155. Open daily, May through September; open weekdays only, the rest of the year. Directions and information are also available from the rangers.

Directions: From I-5, follow SR 530 east for 31 miles to Darrington. From the main intersection turn right and follow SR 20 (Mountain Loop Road) for 10 miles past the junction with road SR 22 to where White Chuck Road (SR 23) comes in on the left (east). Follow this one-lane road 10.3 miles to a large parking area. Trail #643 leads off to the right of the information board at the parking area.

The trail: Trail #634 begins easily, then becomes more strenuous with two series of steep switchbacks. The trail crosses several rivulets and foot-log bridges. When it opens up in a very rocky creekbed, continue straight although the trail seems to disappear. Just past the creekbed, a sign on a tree directs you to Pacific Crest Trail #639 sharply to the left or straight ahead to Kennedy Hot Springs. (Note this sign, it is easy to follow the Pacific Crest Trail by mistake on the way back.)

Continue to a clearing, bearing right toward the river. After crossing a narrow foot-log bridge, take the right fork of the trail, passing signs to a horse camp and pit toilet. Continue a short distance to "Kennedy Cottage." From the cabin, follow the trail to the right. After crossing a bridge over the creek, follow left fork of the trail a few steps to the hot pool.

Source map: *Mt. Baker-Snoqualmie National Forest.*
GPS: N 48.118 W 121.192

WELCOME TO KENNEDY HOT SPRINGS

This popular area has been enjoyed for years by many visitors. It can be enjoyed for years to come with your help.
PLEASE
• Use the map to locate established campsites and toilets.
• Tread lightly on all vegetation and avoid all revegetation areas.
• Leave your campsite free of all food and garbage (including fire rings. Aluminum does not burn).
• Use only down and dead wood and disperse all unused wood.
• The hot spring is located across the bridge and to your left.

Thanks, Darrington Ranger District

203   SCENIC HOT SPRINGS

● **East of the town of Skykomish**

A delightful series of wooden soaking boxes with a spectacular view, located on a steep hillside above the Tyee River in the Mt. Baker-Snoqualmie National Forest. Elevation 3,500 feet. Open all year.

Natural mineral water emerges from several springs at 110° and flows through a hose into the smallest of four rectangular, waist-deep soaking tubs lined with plastic. Temperature can be controlled by diverting the inflow hose. The top pool is known as the "Lobster Pool" as it is very hot. Outflow from this tub flows into the three lower pools where the temperature becomes progressively cooler. An elaborate series of decks, benches, railing, and stairways connect the pools. The apparent local custom is clothing optional.

There are no services except a pit toilet and amenities (such as plastic bags to pack out your trash) to help keep the place pristine at the spring. National Forest campgrounds are along US 2, and it is twenty miles to all other services in Skykomish.

Directions: Off I-5 from Everett, take US 2 about 50 miles southeast to Skykomish. Continue 10 miles until you see the highway bridge spanning the railroad tracks. Across the bridge on your left is mile marker 59. On your right, watch for a primitive powerline road .2 miles east of of the mile marker. Turn right, and unless you have a four-wheel drive, park as soon as possible and walk up the steep rocky road to a clearing where you see a series of powerlines. The dirt road heads up to the clearing where the towers begin and then veers left and up. Before coming to the first set of towers, take the trail that heads off to the right. The trail continues up and rejoins the dirt road at the first set of towers. Continue up the road past 2 more towers and find the final trail heading to the springs shortly after the second tower. From the clearing near tower #7 (look for number plates on the towers), the wide trail S-curves to the southeast. Just past tower #5, on your right, a narrow rocky path arcs uphill through the pines. The trail becomes steeper crossing three seepages on its way to the springs. A heavy gripping rope is tied around trees along two very steep, slippery portions of the trail. Sturdy footgear is recommended.

Note: The springs are on private land within the National Forest. Please respect the property.

Source map: *Mt. Baker-Snoqualmie National Forest* (hot springs not shown on any map).

GPS: N 47.707 W 121.155

> If you have enjoyed soaking at *Scenic,* please send a donation to the group listed below who built and is maintaining the spring for your soaking enjoyment.
> Friends of Scenic Hot Springs,
> PO Box 268, Skykomish, WA 98288

Natural mineral water is obtained from the city water system through an extra pipe that supplies all of the establishments. Restaurants and all other services are a few blocks away in Soap Lake. Elevation is 1,075 feet, with a dry desert temperate climate and a claim of 300 days of sunshine a year.

204A   NOTARAS LODGE
242 Main St. E.   **509 246-0462**
■ **Soap Lake, WA 98851**

Beautiful spruce log lodge with in-room jet tubs and a public bathhouse. Open all year.

Five of the units are equipped with in-room jet tubs built for two. All rooms have an extra spigot over the bathtub to supply hot mineral water. There is also a bathhouse building containing two private-space, old-fashioned, single bathtubs supplied with mineral water. The bathhouse facilities are available to the public (for a fee) as well as to registered guests.

Massage is available on the premises. Visa and MasterCard are accepted.

204B   LAKE MOTEL
322 Daisy S.   **509 246-1611**
■ **Soap Lake, WA 98851**

Large, older downtown motel on main highway.

Twenty-three motel units with double plumbing (city water and mineral water); kitchenettes available. There is also an outdoor hot tub filled with electrically heated tap water as well as a hot or dry sauna. Visa and MasterCard accepted.

204C   TOLO VISTA MOTEL
22 Daisy N. Hwy 17   **509 246-1512**
■ **Soap Lake, WA 98851**

Motel and cottages located opposite the lake on the east end of the beach. Open al year.

All motel and cottage baths are provided with double plumbing, either city water or Soap Lake mineral water, to bathe in.

The six rooms have TVs, kitchens, air conditioning, and microwaves.

204D   THE INN AT SOAP LAKE
226 Main Ave. E.   **509 246-1132**
■ **Soap Lake, WA 98851**

Originally built in 1905 of round river rock. Completely renovated in 1993 with beautifully landscaped grounds and its own private beach right on on Soap Lake. Open all year

A delightful Victorian setting of twenty rooms, a bridal suite, and five cottages. Each room has a fresh-water shower and large mineral water soaking tub. Bridal suite has a whirlpool tub. There is also an indoor pool and hot tub. All have their own patio and barbeque. Rooms are handicap accessible.

Kitchenettes, microwaves, and refrigerators are provided. Massage is available by reservation. Paddleboats and canoes are available for rent. Fishing, hunting, golfing, and bicycling are available nearby. Major credit cards are accepted.

Photos by Phil Wilcox

205 CARSON HOT SPRINGS RESORT
■ PO Box 370   509 427-8292
   Carson, WA 98610

Picturesque, historic resort that prides itself on having used the same bath methods for over 100 years. Elevation 300 feet. Open all year.

Natural mineral water flows out of a spring at 126° and is piped to men's and women's bathhouses. There are eight claw-footed enamel tubs in the men's bathhouse and nine in the women's. Temperature is controllable in each tub, which is drained and filled after each use, requiring no chemical treatment. An attendant, who is with you at all times, applies a sweat wrap after the soak. Bathing suits are not required in the bathhouses, which are available to the public (for a fee) as well as to registered guests.

Television, radio, and telephones are not available on the premises. Massage, restaurant, hotel rooms, cabins, overnight camping, and RV hookups are available. Reservations are a must. A store and service station are within two miles. Hiking and fishing are nearby. Visa and MasterCard are accepted.

Directions: From the intersection of WA 14 and Bridge of the Gods over the Columbia River, go east on WA 14 and watch for signs. Phone for rates, reservations, and further directions if necessary.

206 ST. MARTINS ON THE WIND

● On Carson H.S. Resort property

Small riverbank soaking pools 100 yards below a waterfall on the Wind River at the end of a sometimes difficult scramble over rocks and boulders. Elevation 150 feet. Open all year. The St. Martin family charges a small fee for parking and use of the pools.

Natural mineral water flows out of several seeps at 107° into shallow, sandy-bottom pools at the river's edge. Moving rocks to admit river water cools the pools. The apparent custom is clothing optional.

There are no services available on the premises, but overnight parking is not prohibited at the parking area. A rustic cabin is available for rent. A restaurant, rooms, and bathhouses are available within one mile at the Carson Hot Springs Resort. It is eight miles to campgrounds in the Gifford Pinchot National Forest and fifteen miles to all other services in Hood River.

Directions: As you enter "Home Valley," just east of the Wind River crossing on Hwy 14 (east of Carson), turn left (north) to Berge Road. Drive .7 miles to Julian Cabin Road and turn left. Continue under power pole. Road turns to gravel and dead ends at parking area. A posted sign gives instructions for hiking from there to the springs and for paying the required fee. Sandals and shorts are not recommended as the .5-mile walk is mostly on slippery rocks, and poison oak is abundant.

GPS: N 45.44.19 W 121.48.19

Wellspring describes itself as the "woodland spa at Mount Rainier" and they are as close as you can come to a mineral water soak in semi-wilderness surroundings that are still near the city.

207 WELLSPRING
Star Route   360 569-2514
❏   Ashford, WA 98304

A charming, rustic woodland spa located in a wooded area with a spring-fed pond just outside the southwest entrance to Mt. Rainier National Park. Open all year.

There are two cedar hot tubs, one adjoining a pond overlooking a lush forest setting, and one in a private Japanese garden. Each has its own enclosed building with shower and bathroom facilities. Water temperatures are maintained at 104-106° using propane-heated spring water treated with chlorine. Clothing is optional in private spaces.

Facilities include wood-fired cedar saunas and three cozy log cabins. Breakfast basket included with cabin rental. Massage therapy is available on the premises. Visa and MasterCard are accepted. Phone for rates, reservations, and directions.

208 TOWN TUBS AND MASSAGE
115 Olympia Ave. NE   360 943-2200
❏   Olympia, WA 98501

Modern rent-a-tub establishment in downtown Olympia, two blocks from Percival Landing on Puget Sound.

Private-space hot pools with cedar decks are for rent to the public, using gas-heated tap water treated with chlorine. There are five indoor pools with the water temperature adjustable from 95-104°. Each unit has piped in music .

Therapeutic massage is available on the premises. Visa and MasterCard are accepted. Phone for rates, reservations, and directions.

209 ELLIOTT BAY SAUNA AND HOT TUB CO.
32510 Pacific Hwy. So.   253 952-6154
❏   Federal Way, WA 98003

Plants, dimmer switches and sky lights lend atmosphere to this urban rent-a-tub. Open all year.

Private-space hot pools using chlorine-treated tap water are for rent to the public by the hour. Ten indoor wooden tubs are maintained at temperatures from 101-105°. Each unit contains a sauna. Choose your own music from a large satellite system.

Credit cards are accepted. Phone for rates and directions (no reservations necessary).

Photos by Phil Wilcox

210 GOLDMYER HOT SPRINGS
202 N. 85th St. #106　　206 789-5631
■ **Seattle, WA 98103**

Very remote and beautiful mountain hot springs being preserved by a nonprofit volunteer organization. Prior reservations are required, two weeks in advance to avoid overcrowding. Directions are provided with reservations. (A $10 contribution is requested for each adult.) Elevation 1,800 feet. Open all year.

Natural mineral water flows into an old horizontal mine shaft at temperatures up to 120°. A dam has been built across the mouth of the shaft, creating a combination steam bath and soaking pool with water temperatures up to 109°. The mineral water also falls into several nearby rock-and-cement soaking pools where the temperature is cooler in each lower pool. No pets, fires, smoking, no alcohol, drugs, glass, weapons, or soap are allowed. Clothing policy is determined by the caretaker based on the wishes of those present.

The twenty-mile road to the springs is very rough and the springs are a half-mile hike from the nearest parking. Overnight camping is available on the premises. It is twenty-eight miles to all other services. Access roads vary in quality from Forest Service Class A to Class D, (not suitable for trailers, motor homes and low-clearance vehicles). Ask for a current report on weather and road conditions when phoning for reservations and directions.

You can support the work of this organization by sending tax-deductible contributions to Goldmyer Hot Springs/Northwest Wilderness Programs, 202 N. 85th, #106, Seattle, WA 98103.

Advance reservations are a necessity at *Goldmeyer Hot Springs*. However, they do insure that you will enjoy your soak without too many people around.

211 TUBS SEATTLE
4750 Roosevelt Way NE　　206 527-8827
❏ **Seattle, WA 98105**

Large, modern, pool-rental facility located in the University district of Seattle.

Private, luxurious hot pools are for rent to the public, using gas-heated tap water treated with chlorine. There are twelve indoor acrylic spas with water temperature maintained at 102-104°.

Each private suite also includes a dry heat sauna, stereo system, intercom, shower, and modern decor. An eleven-bed Sun Salon and a juice bar are also available. TUBS CLUB memberships give members reservation privileges and discounts. Visa, MasterCard, and American Express are accepted. Phone for rates and directions.

212   OLYMPIC HOT SPRINGS
(see map)

● **South of Port Angeles**

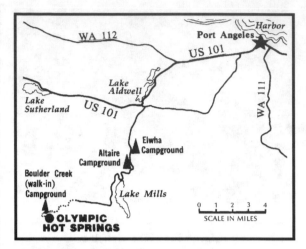

Several user-friendly, primitive springs surrounded by a lush rain forest at the end of a two-mile hike in Olympic National Park. Elevation 1,600 feet. Open all year.

Natural mineral water flows out of several springs at temperatures ranging from 100-112°. Volunteers have built a series of rock-and-sand soaking pools that permit the water to cool down to comfortable soaking temperatures. The hottest pools are those furthest from the creek. Official notices prohibiting nudity are posted often and promptly torn down, resulting in considerable uncertainty. Rangers have been observed issuing a citation only after someone complained and bathers didn't heed orders to dress. However, rangers have not made special trips to the area for the purpose of harassment.

There are no services on the premises, but there is a walk-in campground within 200 yards. It is eight miles to a cafe, store, and service station, seven miles to to Elwha Campground, five and one-half miles to the town of Altaire, and twenty miles to a motel and RV hookups.

Directions: From the city of Port Angeles, go 10 miles west on Olympic Springs Road, turn south and follow signs to Elwha Valley. Paid admission to the National park is required. Continue south 10.3 miles on paved road as it winds up Boulder Creek Canyon to where the road ends. Park and walk the remaining 2.2 miles on the damaged paved road to the old end-of-road parking area. At the west end of that parking area is a quite visible path that brings you to a bridge across Boulder Creek and into the hot-springs area. Most, but not all, paths indicate the presence of a nearby spring.

Conscientious visitors have kept the area litter-free. Please do your part to maintain this standard.

Source map: *NPS Olympic National Park* (hot springs not shown).

GPS: N 47.977 W 123.682

Photo by Jayson Loam

Photos by Phil Wilcox

Courtesy of Sol Duc Hot Springs

Photo by Jayson Loam

213   SOL DUC HOT SPRINGS RESORT

PO Box 2169   360 327-3583
■ Port Angeles, WA 98362

Modernized, historic resort surrounded by the ever-green forest of Olympic National Park. Elevation 1,600 feet. Open daily mid-May through mid-September; weekends only in April and October.

Natural mineral water flows out of a spring at 128° and is piped to a heat exchanger, where the spring water heats the shower water and chlorine-treated cold water swimming pool. The cooled mineral water is then piped to a large soaking pool and two small pools that are maintained at 99-105° on a flow-through basis, requiring no chemical treatment of the water. Two pools are equipped with access ramps for the convenience of disabled persons. All pools are available to the public as well as to registered guests. Bathing suits are required.

Locker rooms, a full-service restaurant, poolside deli, gift shop, convenience store, massage, cabins and RV hookups are available on the premises. It is one-quarter mile to a National Park campground and thirty miles to a service station. MasterCard, American Express, Discover, and Visa are accepted.

Directions: From US 101, two miles west of Fairholm, take Sol Duc Hot Springs Road 12 miles south to the resort.

214   DOE BAY VILLAGE RESORT

Orcas Island Star Rt. 86
                    360 376-2291
■ Olga, WA 98279

Fantastic combination of running streams, waterfalls, and hot mineral water tubs outdoors on a deck with a spectacular view. Elevation sea level. Open all year.

Natural mineral water is pumped out of a well at 45°, heated by electricity, and piped to two outdoor pools, that are surrounded by trees and adjacent to a running stream with waterfalls. The pool water is continuously filtered, treated with chlorine, and exchanged daily. Each pool is large enough for a dozen people, and one of them has hydrojets. Both are maintained at 101-104°, and a third pool contains cool water at air temperature. The wood-fired sauna is large enough for twenty people. The pools and sauna are available to the public as well as to registered guests. Bathing suits are optional.

Massage, vegetarian meals, general store, rustic cabins, overnight camping, RV hookups, and a hostel-type dormitory are available on the premises. Guided kayak trips and hikes in Moran State Park are nearby. It is eleven miles to a store and service station. All major credit cards are accepted.

Directions: Drive onto the Anacortes Ferry which will take you to Orcas Island (about one hour). Go north on Horseshoe Highway for 20.3 miles through Eastsound and Olga to the resort sign for Doe Bay at the east end of island. This very scenic drive takes about one hour.

OREGON

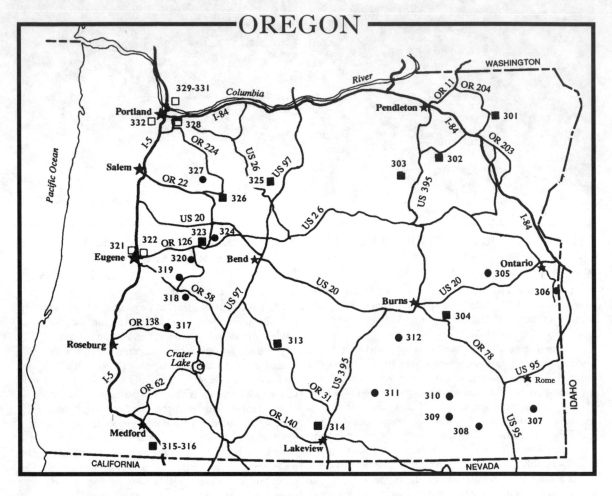

This map was designed to be used with a standard highway map.

MAP SYMBOLS

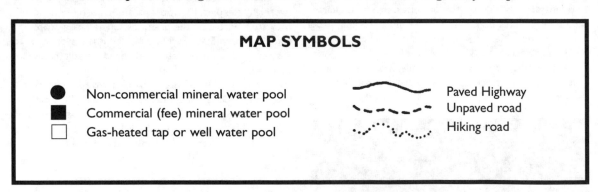

● Non-commercial mineral water pool
■ Commercial (fee) mineral water pool
□ Gas-heated tap or well water pool

Paved Highway
Unpaved road
Hiking road

Photo by Phil Wilcox

Courtesy of Cove Warm Springs Pool

301   COVE WARM SPRINGS POOL
■   **907 Water St.   541 568-4890**
    Cove, OR 97824

Large swimming pool and picnic grounds in the foothills of the Wallowa Mountains. Elevation 3,200 feet. Open May 1 through Labor Day.

Natural mineral water at 86° flows up from a hot spring in the gravel bottom of the pool. Thanks to this continual flow-through, no chlorine is added. Bathing suits are required.

Picnic grounds and snack bar are available on the premises. It is two blocks to a cafe, store, and service station and fifteen miles to a motel. No credit cards are accepted.

Directions: From I-84 in La Grande, take OR 82 exit and go east to OR 237, then 14 miles south to the town of Cove.

302   LEHMAN HOT SPRINGS
    PO Box 187   541 427-3015
■   **Ukiah, OR 97880**

Historic, major hot spring being developed into a large destination resort, located in the beautiful Blue Mountains of Eastern Oregon surrounded by the 3.9 million acre Wallowa-Whitman and Umatilla National Forests. Elevation 4,300 feet. Open all year.

Natural mineral water flows out of several springs at temperatures up to 167° and is mixed with cold creek water before being piped to a series of outdoor pools. The first pool ranges from 112-120°, the second pool ranges from 102-110°, and the swimming pool ranges from 85-90° in the summer and from 90-96° in the winter. A new 9,000 square foot natural hot mineral pool has been added with temperatures ranging from 55-75°. All pools operate on a flow-through basis. The pools are available to the public as well as to registered guests. Bathing suits are required.

Lodging (log cabins, tepees), dressing rooms, mineral water showers, snack bar, game room, RV hookups, camping, and hiking trails are available on the premises. Fishing, cross country skiing, mountain biking, and snowmobiling are available nearby. A store, service station, and motel are located eighteen miles away in Ukiah. Major credit cards are accepted.

Future development plans call for more cabins, hotel/restaurant, home sites, and a small air strip. Phone for status of construction.

Directions: From La Grande, drive eight miles west on I-84 to OR 244, then west for 35 miles. Watch for Lehman Hot Springs signs. From Ukiah, take OR 244 18 miles east to the hot springs exit.

Photo by Justine Hill

Photos by Jayson Loam

303 RITTER HOT SPRINGS
(summer) 541 421-3846
(winter) 509 525-4246

■ Ritter, OR 97872

Historic 1850's stage stop and mineral springs, located in the high desert of Eastern Oregon, along the Middle Fork of the John Day River, between Malheur and Umatilla National Forests. Operated by the Seventh Day Adventists. Elevation 2485 feet. Open for overnight and day use Memorial Day through Labor Day.

A 106° artesian mineral spring on the property (reached via a hanging bridge) emerges into an enclosed cement source pool, then flows by gravity to three private four-foot by four-foot by three-foot deep enclosed private tubs which hold two-to-four people, and into one three-four square roofless enclosed tub. Tubs are maintained at approximately 101°. The pools operate on a flow-through basis so no chemical treatment is necessary. The tubs are drained and cleaned three-to-four times a week. No bathing suits are required in the private tubs. Suits are required in the large outdoor mineral water swimming pool which is maintained at approximately 80°. The pool is closed Friday and Saturday when it is drained, hot-pressure cleaned and refilled. The spilloff from the pool goes into the river, a refreshing place to cool off. The swimming pool is handicap accessible with assistance.

Facilities include eight rooms in the old hotel with a shared bath, two eight-to-ten person cabins, RV and tenting spots, and a picnic area with barbeque grills and 100-year-old white poplar and locust trees for shade. There is also river rafting and fishing for trout and squaw fish. Many of the other buildings are currently undergoing renovations. Gas, provisions, and other services are available thirteen miles away in long Creek. No credit cards accepted.

Directions: From US 395 13 miles north of Long Creek, and 13 miles south of Dale, drive west for 10 miles on Grant County Rd. 15 which follows the Middle Fork of the John Day River. Turn right on gravel County Rd. 38 for .3 miles to the resort.

304 CRYSTAL CRANE HOT SPRINGS
(see map on page 65)
HC 73-2653 Hwy 78   541 493-2312

■ Burns, OR 97720

A growing, 160-acre resort in the wide-open spaces of the eastern Oregon high desert. Cranes, avocets, and other birds often visit the pond. Elevation 4,200 feet. Open all year.

Natural mineral water flows out of several springs at 185° and supplies six private-space tubs where hot and cold mineral water valves are controlled by the customer to obtain the desired temperature. The mineral water also fills a large, 90-foot pond where temperatures range from 95-105°. All the pools operate on a flow-through basis so that no chemical treatment of the water is necessary. Most facilities are handicap accessible. Bathing suits are not required in the private tub rooms.

Facilities include cabins, RV park, and a tent camping area. A small snack bar and microwave are available. It is two and one-half miles to the nearest restaurant in Crane and twenty-five miles to all other services in Burns. Credit cards accepted.

Directions: From Burns, drive 25 miles east on Hwy 78 and watch for signs.

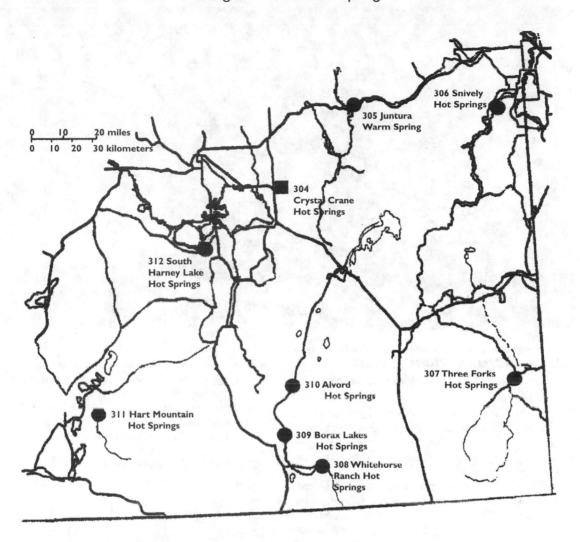

306 Snively
Hot Springs

305 Juntura
Warm Spring

0   10   20 miles
0   10   20   30 kilometers

304
Crystal Crane
Hot Springs

312 South
Harney Lake
Hot Springs

307 Three Forks
Hot Springs

310 Alvord
Hot Springs

311 Hart Mountain
Hot Springs

309 Borax Lakes
Hot Springs

308 Whitehorse
Ranch Hot
Springs

Photos by Chris Andrews

305   JUNTURA WARM SPRING
(see map on page 65)

● **Northeast of the town of Juntura**

A series of pools located on an island in the Malheur River surrounded by the rolling hills of the east Oregon desert. Elevation 3,000 feet. Open all year, depending on snowfall and river level.

Natural mineral water feeds directly into a large, sixteen by thirty-five foot pool, two-to-four feet deep at a temperature of 115°. A small deck and benches offer a place to eat lunch and enjoy the scenery. The hot water continues its flow down to a four by eighteen-foot pool at the edge of the Malheur River. Cold water can be added to the top pool with a bucket (bring it along), and to the lower pool by moving the rocks to let in the river water. A word of caution: the top pool may never be cool enough to soak in. Be careful. Suits are optional.

There are no services on the premises. Public and private campgrounds are within six miles and all other services are approximately two miles away in Juntura.

Directions: From Juntura travel east on US 20 until you see a bridge at about milepost 92. Before crossing the bridge turn left (north) on a small road. At .1 mile turn right and cross the river on another bridge which runs parallel and just north of the US 20 bridge. During good weather and when the water level is low you can bear left

after crossing the bridge .5 miles and drive directly to the spring. At high water the spring is located on an island and you can drive only until where the road is flooded, park, and wade the river to the island. The spring is visible from the road approximately 100-150 yards to the left.

Source maps: Oregon Geothermal ML 54 (Warm Spring; Beulah (15 minutes).

GPS: N 43.77615 W 118.04808

Photos by Justine Hill

The federal lands around *Snively* are administered by the Bureau of Land Management and have been designated a "watchable wildlife area." The canyon is home to a wide variety of frogs, reptiles, deer, bobcats, river otters, beaver, weasels, and multiple species of birds, including eagles, hawks, owls, herons, egrets, and ducks.

306   SNIVELY HOT SPRINGS

(see map on page 65)

● **Southwest of the town of Owyhee**

Easily accessible, primitive hot spring on the river's edge in the Owyhee River canyon. Elevation 2,400 feet. Open all year.

Natural mineral water flows out of several springs and a concrete standpipe at temperatures of more than 150° and then flows toward the river where volunteers have built several rock-and-sand soaking pools. The temperature in the pools is controlled by varying the amount of cold river water permitted to enter. The pools are visible from the road, so bathing suits are advisable although the common consent of those present seems to prevail.

Services include a BLM-built outhouse with a chemical toilet, trash receptacles, and a large dirt parking and camping area shaded by a few trees. It is 10 miles to a cafe, store, and service station and 18 miles to a motel and RV hookups.

Directions: From the town of Owyhee, on OR 201, follow signs west toward Owyhee Lake and State Park. When the road enters Owyhee Canyon look for a large, metal water pipe running up the steep slopes on both sides of the road. Go 1.4 miles beyond that metal pipe and look on the river side of the road for a large stone and cement outhouse and a large dirt parking area.

Source map: USGS *Owyhee Dam, Oregon.*
GPS: N 43.727 W 117.203

307   THREE FORKS HOT SPRINGS
(see map on page 65)

● **Southeast of the city of Rome**

Two small pools on the east side of the river and a gem of a secluded pool and waterfall on the other. Located in the upper Owyhee River Canyon, south of Jordan Valley, with spectacular sunsets visible from springs and nearby campground. Elevation 4,000 feet. Open all year; wet weather may make roads impassable, and high water makes it dangerous to ford the river.

Natural mineral water flows at 95° from several sets of springs on the east bank and winds its way through the grass toward the river and into two small pools. On the west bank, several showers cascade 95° water into a beautifully clear, gravel-bottom pool. The prevailing custom is clothing optional. The entire creek that produces the waterfalls is warm and there are dozens of soaking opportunities up the creek.

It is three miles to Three Forks, a primitive BLM campground, and fifty-one miles to all other services in Rome.

Directions: From Rome, proceed 18.2 miles east on OR 95 to milepost 36. Turn right (south) on excellent gravel road Consider this point 0. At 7.4 miles bear right, at 8.3 miles bear left, at 16.7 miles bear left, at 28.6 miles bear right, and at 31.4 miles you are on a bluff looking down into the valley. At 32.8 miles there is a "T". The campground is 2.8 miles to the right. Turn left to the springs and at 33.2 there is a wooden bridge. Cross the bridge and at 33.4 bear left at the "T". The road from here is very steep and rocky (You may want to consider walking the remaining 2.2 miles.) At 35.4 miles there is a small, steep pullout in the rocks where 2-3 vehicles may park. Two small pools are located on the hillside below the road across from the turnout. The majority of the pools are located on the other side of the river above the waterfalls. At 35.6 miles the road ends near the river where you would cross and walk up to the springs. Trailers and motorhomes not recommended. High clearance, four-wheel drive vehicles are best.

Note: The springs are on private, unposted land. Please take particular care to leave nothing but footprints.

GPS: N 42.53007 W 117.18447

If you (and your vehicle) are up to it, you may have the opportunity to have a private soak in one of the many pools at the end of the trail.

Photos by Chris Andrews

Photo by Chris Andrews

308   WHITEHORSE RANCH HOT SPRING
(see map on page 65)

●   **South of the town of Fields**

A very remote, primitive hot spring requiring about twenty-six miles of unpaved road travel in the dry, southeastern corner of Oregon in the Alvord Desert. Elevation 4,000 feet. Open all year.

Natural mineral water at 114° bubbles up through the bottom of a volunteer-built, twelve-foot sandy-bottomed soaking pool that is about eighteen inches deep, crystal clear and ranges in temperature from 104-112°. The overflow runs into a second pool, three to four-feet deep, that ranges in temperature from 70-90°, depending on air temperature and wind conditions. Clothing optional.

There are no services on the premises, but there is plenty of level space on which overnight parking or tenting is not prohibited. A new concrete outhouse was built by, and the area is currently maintained by, the Oregon Dept. of Fish and Wildlife, Vale District BLM. It is forty-five miles to all services in Burns Junction.

Directions: From Burns Junction on US 95, go 21 miles south on US 95, then turn west on a mostly good gravel road and go 21 miles to Whitehorse Ranch. About 2.5 miles past the ranch, where the fence line ends, turn left on well-traveled dirt road. Drive 2.5 miles to the spring. If you miss this road, proceed approximately five miles from the ranch and turn left on a dirt road. Immediately take the left fork. Utility pole on right is B 281. Drive 2.1 miles. Bear right at old cattle loading ramp. Spring is on right, and a new concrete toilet is just past the spring on left.

Coming from Denio junction, NV, drive north on Oregon Harney County Rd 201 for 12 miles. Turn right (east) 8 miles south of Fields and continue on good gravel road 29 miles, following signs to Whitehorse Ranch. Continue with above directions.

Source map: BLM *Southern Malheur.*
GPS: N 42.27570 W 118.26545

Photo by Justine Hill

Photo by Skip Hill

Photo by Justine Hill

309   BORAX LAKES HOT SPRING
(see map on page 65)

● **Northeast of the town of Fields**

In a desert area dotted with hot pools, many too hot to soak in, this last pool on the north end of the ridge finally gets us to a perfect soak in the arid Alvord Desert. Elevation 4,200 feet. Open all year.

Natural mineral comes up through two sources in the bottom of a large pond at 103°. The crystal clear water fills the muddy-bottom pool which is surrounded by a deposit of built-up tufa. Clothing optional.

There is plenty of level ground to camp on. Gas and limited grocery supplies can be found in Fields. The nearest large town northeast of the springs is Burns Junction, approximately fifty miles away. Come prepared with gas, water and supplies–this is the desert.

Directions: From Fields, go north about a mile plus on SR 205 continuing straight on the gravel road that has a sign saying "Highway 78, 62 miles." In .4 of a mile you will notice a power substation on the right with a power line road heading into the desert. Take this road, following the power lines for a few miles until the road turns left. The power line will continue but take the well worn road through a couple of gates and pass Lower Borax Lake. After passing several more gates you will start to see the hot pools. Check the temperature of each one until you find the one that's right for you. The one at the end of the road is highly recommended.

310   ALVORD HOT SPRINGS
(see map on page 65)

● **Northeast of the town of Fields**

Funky hot springs pools, formerly a popular bathhouse, located on the vast sandy Alvord Desert area of eastern Oregon, on the east side of Steen Mountains. Elevation 4,000 feet. Open all year.

Hot 116° water with a slight sulfur smell flows out of the ground at various spots along the edge of the hill and into an algae-filled pond in a marshy grasslands along the west side of the desert. From the ponds it flows through a channel to the old bathhouse. One ten-foot by ten-foot by five-foot pool is enclosed in a roofless tin shed along with a separate dressing room. The other pool, almost as large is outdoors. Inflow can be plugged until desired soaking temperature is reached. Pools have plugs for draining and cleaning. Water continually flows through a pipe into the two algae-filled pools and runs off into the desert through a gully. Although the pools are visible from the road bathing suits are not necessary.

There are no services and no shade but plenty of level ground for overnight parking. Gas, groceries, a cafe, motel, propane and an RV park are located in Fields.

Directions: Drive north from Fields on County Rd. 201, a good gravel road, for 25 miles. You'll see the tin shed sitting all by itself in the dry desert lake bed, on the east side of the road.

For your information: McDermitt, a small town on the Oregon-Nevada border has a motel, RV park, country store with gas, and a casino run by the local tribes.

Photo by Justine Hill

Hart Mountain: A cold creek flows under the bridge. The hot pool is inside the enclosure which was erected to keep out the wild animals.

311   HART MOUNTAIN HOT SPRING
(see map on page 65)

● **North of the town of Adel**

Semi-improved hot spring enclosed by a roofless, cement block wall and surrounded by miles of barren plateau within the Hart Mountain National Antelope Refuge. Elevation 6,000 feet. Open all year.

Natural mineral water flows out of a spring at 98°. The edge of the spring has been cemented to create a soaking pool that maintains that temperature. The cement block enclosure is built to keep the animals out of the hot pool. The five-foot by ten-foot pool is approximately five-feet deep has an uneven rock bottom, and a set of stairs which makes it handicap accessible with assistance. There is no posted clothing policy, which leaves it up to the mutual consent of those present. A sign says "Nude bathers must lock door." (No one does.)

There are no services available on the premises, but there is an abundance of level ground on which overnight parking is not prohibited. It is twenty miles to a cafe and store and forty miles to all other services in Adel. Hart Mt. Headquarters visitors room is open 24 hours for maps, brochures, wilderness permits. Just past the Headquarters, a sign directs you to the hot springs.

Note: The last seven miles of gravel road is very steep. Carry plenty of water for you and your vehicle.

Source map: *Hart Mountain National Antelope Refuge*.

312   SOUTH HARNEY LAKE HOT SPRINGS
(see map on page 65)

● **South of Burns Junction**

Pool located at the south end of Harney Lake in an area called the Harney Basin surrounded by a large meadow area dotted with lakes and thermal water. Elevation 4,200 feet. Open all year.

Natural mineral water with a great flow meanders down through the grasses in a small channel and is diverted into two pools. The upper pool is too hot to soak in. The water cools from 109° as it fills the lower pool which is about ten feet around and two to three-feet deep. The pool might be handicap accessible with assistance. Bathing suits would be handy on busy weekends.

There is plenty of level ground and places for camping. All services are 34 miles away in Burns.

Directions: From Burns head south on OR 205. .9 miles south of mile marker 23 turn west onto South Harney Road. continue west 8.2 miles to the fork and bear right. The springs are .2 of a mile further on.

Source map: Oregon Geothermal (HA 64).
GPS: N 43.18038 W 119.05794

Photo by Chris Andrews

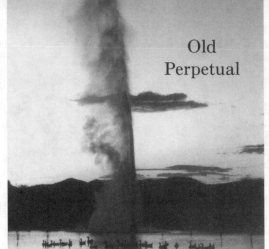
Old Perpetual

Courtesy of Hunter's Hot Spring Resort

Courtesy of Summer Lake

The pool, being refilled here with fresh water, was built in 1927, in on the Historic Register as the oldest spa-related structure in Lake County.

This area is of particular interest to wildlife/bird enthusiasts. Big-horn sheep can be viewed through binoculars from the premises. The Summer Lake Wildlife Refuge, several miles north on Highway 31, is a nesting area for many species of birds.

313   SUMMER LAKE HOT SPRINGS
541 943-3931
■   **Paisley, OR 97636**

Newly landscaped, small, indoor plunge in the wide-open spaces south of Summer Lake located off Hwy 31 which has just been designated a National Scenic Highway. Elevation 4,200 feet. Open all year.

Natural mineral water flows out of a spring at 110° and cools as it is piped to the pool building. Water temperature in the fifteen by thirty-foot indoor pool is maintained at 102° in the winter and 100° in the summer on a continuous flow-through basis that requires no chemical treatment of the water. Bathing suits are required.

Dressing rooms, overnight camping, and RV hookups are available on the premises. Sites are outfitted with grills and picnic tables. Vintage airstream trailers will be available for overnight accommodations. It is six miles to all other services. No credit cards are accepted.

Future improvements will include outdoor pools, some with handicap access. Clothing optional pools, covered picnic shelters, cabins, and facilities for larger groups are planned. Call for status.

Location: Six miles northwest of the town of Paisley on OR 31. Watch for sign on north side of road at mile marker 92.

314   HUNTER'S HOT SPRING RESORT
PO Box 1189   541 947-4142
■   **Lakeview, OR 97630**

Historic spa expanded and remodeled into a destination resort. Located in the rolling southern Oregon hills. Elevation 4.200 feet. open all year.

Natural mineral water flows out of several springs a temperatures up to 203° and into cooling ponds from where it is piped to two outdoor pools and to a heat exchanger for the hot water system in the buildings. "Old Perpetual" hot water geyser erupts approximately every two minutes and flows into large "Goldfish Lake" where it cools. The hydropool is maintained at 105° and the swimming pool around 100°. The pools are drained and cleaned regularly and no chemicals are added. Facilities are handicap accessible with assistance. Bathing suits are required.

A motel, lounge, restaurant, gift shop, hair salon, and massage therapist are on the premises. A weight room and indoor racquetball court are for members only. Hunter's RV Park is right next door. It is one and one-half miles to Lakeview and all other services. Major credit cards accepted.

Location: Two miles north of Lakeview on US 395.

Photo by Justine Hill

Photo by Phil Wilcox

315 LITHIA SPRINGS INN
2165 W. Jackson Rd.   800 482-7128
■ **Ashland, OR 97520**

Built in the country tradition, Lithia Springs Inn, just outside of the charming town of Ashland, is located on a unique geographical wonder—a natural hot spring.

An artesian well pumps hot natural mineral water at 100° into the inn where it is used to fill the in-room whirlpool tubs and provide much of the heating. The water temperature is boosted and the sulphur smell removed from the water.

Besides providing all of the luxurious amenities found at this up-scale Bed and Breakfast, including a bountiful breakfast, you can also order a massage in your room. Major credit cards accepted.

Phone for reservations and directions.

316 JACKSON WELLSPRINGS
2253 Hwy 99 N.   503 482-3776
■ **Ashland, OR 97520**

Jackson WellSprings is in the process of building a sanctuary for mind, body, and spirit. Elevation 1,650 feet. Pool open May 15 to September 30; tubs, cafe, and, camping open all year.

Natural mineral water flows out of three springs at 100-115° and directly into an outdoor swimming pool that is treated with chlorine and maintains a temperature of 84-90°. There are two indoor soaking tubs, one individual tub with jets, and one large enough for two persons, in which heated natural mineral water can be controlled up to 110°. These tubs are drained and cleaned after each use so that no chemical treatment of the water is necessary. There is ramp access to the cafe and pool house with assistance available upon request. Bathing suits are required, except in private soaking rooms. Clothing optional time may be able to be arranged.

Remodeled locker rooms, a garden cafe serving lunch, picnic and play areas, patio area in a garden setting, upgraded, full RV hookups and tent sites, swimming lessons, and professional massages are available on the premises. Summer musical events are presented and parties can be arranged for. All other services are a few miles away in Ashland. Expansion plans include large gardens with medicinal and edible plants, a modern clinic, and varying therapy programs. No credit cards accepted.

Location: Two miles north of Ashland at the Valley View Road exit from US 99.

317 UMPQUA HOT SPRINGS

(see map)

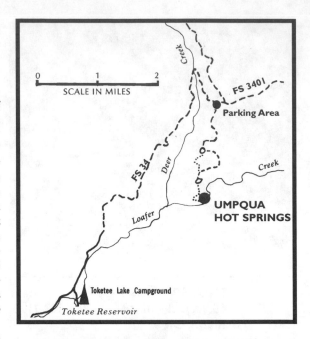

● **Northwest of Crater Lake**

Popular, semi-improved hot spring on a wooded bluff overlooking the North Umpqua River, in the Umpqua National Forest. Elevation 2,600 feet. Open all year.

Natural mineral water flows out of a spring at 108° and is carried by hose directly into a sheltered, six-foot by six-foot pool that volunteers have carved out of the spring-built travertine deposit. The only way to cool the water in the tub is to remove the hose. There is also a very hot upper tub, around 112. Two other volunteer-built rock pools are slightly down hill and somewhat cooler. There are no posted clothing requirements, and the location is quite remote, so a clothing-optional custom would be expected. However, the location is so popular, especially on summer weekends, that it is advisable to take a bathing suit with you. You may have to wait your turn to share a rather crowded pool.

There's an outhouse at the springs and a restroom/changing room at the parking lot. It is three miles to a Forest Service campground and twenty-five miles to all other services.

Directions: Drive 60 miles east of Roseburg on OR 138 to Toketee Junction. Turn north on paved road FS 34 (Toketee Rigdon Road). Drive 2.3 miles, turn right on FS 3401 (Thorn Prairie Road), and drive two miles to the parking area. Walk across the bridge over the North Umpqua River, bear right on the North Umpqua Trail, and climb 1,200 feet east to springs. The first third of the trail is quite steep.

Source map: *Umpqua National Forest.*
GPS: N 43.1750 W 122.2150

Besides providing year-round protection from weather extremes, the shelter helps keep the ubiquitous mosquito away.

Photo by Bob Seal

318   MCCREDIE HOT SPRINGS

● **East of the town of Oakridge**

Easily accessible, primitive hot springs with a strong skinny-dipping tradition, located on the north and south banks of Salt Creek in the Willamette National Forest. Elevation 2,100 feet. Open all year for day use only.

Natural mineral water flows out of several springs on the north bank at 120° and on the south bank at 140°. The water is channeled into a series of shallow, volunteer-built, rock-and-mud pools where it cools as it flows toward the creek. The pools on the south bank tend to be larger and around 100°. There are hot jets on the bottom of the creek, so be careful. Despite the proximity of a main highway, the apparent local custom is clothing optional.

There are no services available on the premises. A large, level parking area permits parking from sunrise to sunset only. It is less than one mile to a Forest Service campground and ten miles to all other services.

Directions: To reach the springs and pools on the north bank drive from the town of Oakridge, drive drive approximately 10 miles east on OR 58 past Blue Pool Campground. At .1 miles past mile marker 45, turn right (south) into a large parking area between the road and the creek. Walk to the upstream (east) end of the parking area and follow a well-worn path 40 yards to the springs.

To reach the springs and soaking pools on the south bank, drive .5 miles east on OR 58, turn right on Shady Gap Road across the bridge, and stay right on FS 5875. Drive .1 miles, park, and look for an overgrown path that follows the creek .25 miles back downstream to the pools.

Photos by Phil Wilcox

GPS: N 43.4220 W 122.1715

319   MEDITATION POOL (WALL CREEK) WARM SPRING

● **Northeast of the town of Oakridge**

Idyllic, primitive warm spring on the wooded banks of Wall Creek at the end of a short, easy trail in the Willamette National Forest. Elevation 2,200 feet. Open all year for day use only.

Natural mineral water flows up through the gravel bottom of a volunteer-built, rock-and-sand pool at 104°. The pool temperature ranges up to 96° depending on air temperature and wind conditions. While the water is not hot enough for therapy soaking, it is ideal for effortless lolling. The apparent local custom is clothing optional.

There are no services available on the premises. It is five miles from the trailhead to a Forest Service campground and nine miles to all other services.

Directions: In Oakridge turn north off OR 58 at stop light. Go over railroad track and turn east (right) onto First St. which becomes FS 24. Nine miles from firehouse, turn (left) north on FS 1934 (sign says "Blair Lake 8 miles") for .5 miles on gravel road and watch for trailhead sign on (left) west side of the road. There is no name or number given for the trail at the trailhead area. Follow a well-worn path along Wall Creek for 600 yards to the creekside pool. Tree sign says "Warm Springs Trail No. 3582."

Source map: *Willamette National Forest.*
GPS: N 43.4806 W 122.1840

Whether you go alone or with friends, this pool provides a delicious warm soak amid ferns and trees, and it is only a short distance from the trail.

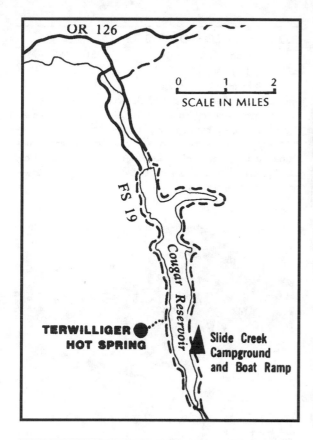

Directions: From OR 126 approximately five miles east of Blue River, turn south on FS 19 along the west side of Cougar Reservoir. The marked hot-springs trailhead is on the west side of the road just past milepost 7 and .3 miles south of Boone Creek. A large parking area is on the east side of the road, .1 miles beyond the trailhead. Parking is permitted from sunrise to sunset only.

Reference map: *Willamette National Forest* (hot springs not shown).

GPS: N 44.083 W 122.233

320   TERWILLIGER (COUGAR) HOT SPRINGS

(see map)

● **Southeast of the town of Blue River**

A lovely series of user-friendly, log-and-stone soaking pools in a picturesque forest canyon at the end of an easy quarter-mile trail in the Willamette National Forest. Elevation 3,000 feet. Open all year for day use only.

Natural mineral water flows out of a spring at 116° and directly into the first of a series of volunteer-built pools, each of which is a few degrees cooler than the one above. Water temperature may vary depending on flow. An organized group of volunteers has also built access steps and railings. The apparent local custom is clothing optional.

There are no services available on the premises. There is a walk-in campground within .5 miles. Overnight parking is prohibited along the road for one mile on both sides of the trailhead. It is four miles to a Forest Service campground and eight miles to all other services.

321 SPRINGFIELD SPAS

1100 Main St. 503 741-1777

❏ Springfield, OR 97477

Well-maintained, suburban, rent-a-tub establishment located on the main street in downtown Springfield.

Private-space hydrojet pools using chlorine-treated tap water are for rent to the public by the hour. Twelve fiberglass tubs in open-roof enclosed spaces are maintained at 102°. Each unit includes a covered dressing area with shower and stereo.

Three tanning beds are available on the premises. Visa, MasterCard and Discover are accepted. Phone for rates, reservations, and directions.

322 ONSEN HOT TUB RENTALS

1883 Garden Ave. 503 345-9048

❏ Eugene, OR 97403

Well-maintained, enclosed, rent-a-tub establishment located near the University of Oregon.

Private-space hydrojet pools using chlorine-treated tap water are for rent to the public by the hour. Fourteen fiberglass tubs in open-roof enclosed spaces are maintained at 102°. Each unit includes a covered dressing area.

No credit cards are accepted. Phone for rates, reservations, and directions.

Photos by Jayson Loam

Photo by Phil Wilcox

323 BELKNAP LODGE AND HOT SPRINGS
59296 Belknap Springs Rd.

541 822-3512

■ **Belknap Springs, OR 97413**

Riverside resort, newly remodeled, and with very attractive grounds, in a wilderness setting surrounded by the lush greenery of Willamette National Forest. Elevation 1,700 feet. Open all year.

Natural mineral water flows out of a spring at 196° and is piped into a combination reservoir and heat exchanger where heat is extracted for space heating and for the hot water supply in the lodge and the RV park. The cooled mineral water is piped to outdoor pools at the lodge and the RV park. Both pools are lightly treated with chlorine and maintained at a temperature of 100-102° in the winter and 100° in the summer. Four lodge rooms have indoor hydrojet tubs controllable up to 110°. These tubs are drained and cleaned after each use so that no chemical treatment of the water is needed. The pools are available to the public as well as to registered guests. Bathing suits are required, except in private rooms.

Four cabins, ten lodge rooms, forty-five tent and RV hookup sites, a snack bar, and bicycle rentals are available on the premises. Arrangements can be made for fishing and white water rafting. It is six miles to all other services. Credit cards accepted. Phone for reservations.

Location: On OR 126, six miles east of the town of McKenzie Bridge. Follow signs.

A new steel bridge takes you across the river to the spring's source and the many hiking trails through the surrounding forest.

Photo by Chris Andrews

Photo by Bob Seal

324   BIGELOW (DEER CREEK) HOT SPRING

● **Northeast of the town of McKenzie Bridge**

A small, rock-and-sand pool in a fern-lined grotto on the McKenzie River. Elevation 2,000 feet. Open all year.

A small flow of natural mineral water (130°) bubbles up from the bottom of a volunteer-dug pool, maintaining a comfortable 102-104° soaking temperature. The apparent local custom is clothing optional.

There are no services available on the premises. It is 1.5 miles to a campground (Ollalie), three miles to a motel and RV hookups (Belknap Hot Springs), and six miles to all other services.

Directions: From the town of McKenzie Bridge, drive nine miles northeast on OR 126. Drive .4 miles past milepost 15, then turn left onto FS 2654 (Deer Creek Road). Park just beyond the bridge over the McKenzie River. Follow the signed McKenzie River Trail a short way south and watch for the second faint path heading down the steep bank to the pool at the river's edge.

GPS: N 44.1422 W 122.0330

Whoever has jurisdiction here at the springs has mandated that the springs are only to be open from sunrise to sunset. A hefty fine ensues for those caught using the spring after dark. While this may seem harsh, it is often the only way that the springs can be protected from those who wish to use it as a "party spot," and do not haul away their trash, and generally abuse the springs. This rule is certainly better than closing the springs altogether. Please cooperate so that the spring may remain open.

Photo by Phil Wilcox

325 KAH-NEE-TA RESORT

PO Box K   503 553-1112
Warm Springs, OR 97761

Full destination resort with lodge, golf course, and gaming casino, all owned and operated by the Confederated Tribes of the Warm Springs Indian Reservation. In these foothills on the east side of the Cascade Mountains, the sun shines 300 days a year. Elevation 1,500 feet. Open all year.

Natural mineral water flows out of a spring from the Warm Spring River at 140° and is covered as it flows to the bathhouse and large village swimming pool which is maintained at a temperature of 95° and to two spas at 103°. Pool and tubs treated with chlorine. The large pool at the lodge is unheated tap water. The men's and women's bathhouses each contain five tiled Roman tubs in which the soaking temperature is individually controlled up to 110°. Tubs are drained and filled after each use. Multiple hot tubs at 103° are to be found all over the grounds. Pools and bathhouses are available to the public as well as to registered guests. Many areas are handicap accessible. Bathing suits are required in public areas.

A European health and beauty spa features massage, reflexology, body treatments. Hydrotherapy tubs, saunas, and steambaths are also available. The resort boasts snack bars, delis and restaurant, a championship eighteen-hole golf course, volleyball and basketball courts, hiking, biking, horse and trails, and a gaming casino. Camping spaces, tepees, and full RV hook-ups are available in the village area. It is eleven miles to a store and service station. All major credit cards accepted.

Directions: From US 26 in Warm Springs, follow signs 11 miles northeast to resort.

Kah-Nee-Ta caters to 5,000 guest per day at this fully equipped resort that can provide space for a huge convention or offer a night's stay in a tepee. The focal point of the 600,000-acre reservation is the Museum at Warm Springs —Oregon's first Native American museum.

326 BREITENBUSH HOT SPRINGS
RETREAT AND CONFERENCE CENTER
PO Box 578   503 854-3314
■ **Detroit, OR 97342**

This rustic retreat has been renovated by the intentional community that operates it as a worker-owned cooperative. The resort is located on the banks of the Breitenbush River, surrounded by the Willamette National Forest. Elevation 2,300 feet. Open all year; with periodic closed camps.

Natural mineral water flows out of springs and artesian wells at temperatures up to 180°. Four covered outdoor soaking tubs use flow-through mineral water requiring no chemical treatment. Each is maintained at a different temperature ranging from 60-111°. Three outdoor pools in a sacred meadow overlooking the river operate on a flow-through basis with temperatures averaging between 100-110°depending on weather conditions. The sauna house sits atop a 180° mineral spring. Tubs and pools are available to the public for day use as well as to overnight guests, but prior reservations are strongly advised. Clothing is optional in the tubs and sauna area unless a workshop leader requests special swimsuit-required times.

Massage, hydrotherapy, and aromatherapy, as well as vegetarian meals, and cabins are available on the premises. Daily well-being programs such as yoga and ecstatic dance, are offered without charge.

It is eleven miles to a store, service station and phone, one and one-half miles to overnight camping, and seventy miles to RV hookups. Organizations and individuals are invited to request rates for facilities suitable for seminars and conferences. Visa and MasterCard are accepted.

Location: Eleven miles northeast of Detroit. Phone for rates, reservations, and directions.

Whether you attend an educational healing seminar or a mushroom hunt, *Breitenbush Hot Springs* with its access to the river—and several tubs to view it from—offers an ideal place to relax and enjoy nature.

Courtesy of Breitenbush Hot Springs

Besides the springs by the river, there are several other spiritual and relaxing places to soak.

Photo by Leigh Springer

327   BAGBY HOT SPRINGS

● **Southeast of the town of Estacada**

One of the best: a well-planned rustic facility featuring hot mineral water supplied through a 150-foot log flume. A lush rain forest and tumbling mountain stream make the 1.5 mile access trail enjoyable in its own right. Elevation 2,200 feet. Open all year.

Natural mineral water emerges from two springs at 135° and is flumed to an outdoor, round cedar tub on a deck at the upper spring site and to two bathhouse buildings at the lower springs. The partially-roofed bathhouse is a replica of the one that burned down in 1979 and offers five hand-hewn cedar tubs in private rooms. The open-sided bathhouse offers a single communal space containing three hewn tubs and a round cedar tub. A flume diversion gate at each tub brings in more hot water whenever desired. All tubs are drained and cleaned daily so no chemical treatment of the water is necessary. There are no posted clothing requirements, and the apparent custom in the communal bathhouse is clothing optional.

All facilities are made possible and are managed by the Friends of Bagby Hot Springs, Inc., a non-profit volunteer organization operating under a special use permit with the Forest Service to restore, preserve, and maintain the area. Volunteers also serve as hosts for the public. You can support this pioneering organization by sending tax-deductible contributions to Friends of Bagby, Inc., PO Box 1798, Clackamas, OR 97015-1798.

There is a picnic area on the premises, but no overnight camping is permitted. A walk-in campground is located at Shower Creek, one-third of a mile beyond Bagby. A drive-in Forest Service Campground (Nohorn) is located adjacent to the trailhead parking area, and the Pegleg Falls Campground is located one-half mile northeast of the trailhead. All other services are available thirty-two miles away in Estacada.

Photo by Tom Paulu

A network of wood flumes and pipes carries the hot water to the individually controlled tubs in the bathhouse—a replica of the one that burned down in the 1970s. The half roof seems to be slanted in such a way as to keep the sun off in summer and the snow away in winter. The walk in through an absolutely gorgeous forest and along fern-lined streams only adds to the anticipated pleasure of a delightful soak.

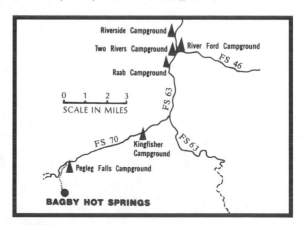

Riverside Campground
Two Rivers Campground
River Ford Campground
FS 46
Raab Campground
FS 63
0 1 2 3
SCALE IN MILES
FS 70
Kingfisher Campground
FS 63
Pegleg Falls Campground
BAGBY HOT SPRINGS

328 FOUR SEASONS HOT TUBBING
19059 SE Division   503 666-3411
❑   Gresham, OR 97030

Attractive, suburban rent-a-tub facility featuring enclosed outdoor tubs. Open all year.

Private-space hot pools using chlorine-treated tap water are for rent to the public by the hour. The six enclosed, outdoor fiberglass hydrojet pools are maintained at a temperature of 104°. Each unit includes indoor dressing room, shower, and toilet.

Visa and MasterCard are accepted. Phone for rates, reservations, and directions.

Photo by Phil Wilcox

Photo by Jayson Loam

329   OPEN AIR HOT TUBBING
11126 NE Halsey   503 257-8191
❑   Portland, OR 97220

Unique, suburban rent-a-tub featuring open-roofed wood patios. Open all year.

Private-space hot pools using chlorine-treated tap water are for rent to the public by the hour. Six enclosed, outdoor fiberglass hydrojet pools are maintained at temperatures ranging from 102-104°. Each unit has an outdoor water spray over the pool and an indoor dressing room with shower and toilet. Three of the units can be combined to accommodate a party of twenty-four. There is a sauna in one unit.

AM/FM cassettes, cable television, VCR in two rooms, and a sauna are available for use. An open-air tanning salon is also on the premises. Visa and MasterCard are accepted. Phone for rates, reservations, and directions.

Inner City Hot Tubs attempts to provide a full repertoire of classes and services for people who are into relaxation, healing, and growth.

330   INNER CITY HOT TUBS, COMMON GROUND WELLNESS CENTER

2927 NE Everett   503 238-1065
❏   Portland, OR 97232

Open-air, family-style pools and sauna in a garden setting near downtown Portland. This non-profit community corporation offers classes in health and relaxation.

Two communal hydrojet pools, cold pool (summer only), flotation tanks, sauna, and sun deck are for rent to the public by the hour. Both hot pools use gas-heated tap water treated with chlorine and are maintained at 104°. Bathing suits are optional in the pool and sauna areas.

Hakomi therapy, yoga, massage, child care, homeopathy, rebirthing, and acupressure are available on the premises. No credit cards are accepted. Phone for rates, reservations, and directions.

331   PORTLAND TUB AND TAN

8028 SE Stark St.   503 261-1180
❏   Portland, OR 97215

Downtown facility with hi-tech, computerized water chemistry located in the commercial district off the Stark St. exit from the 205 freeway. Open all year.

Four tubs in private, air-conditioned rooms offer computerized water chemistry for your safety, a restroom, shower and towels in each room, and DMX stereo for your enjoyment. The tubs are completely sanitized after each use and the water is chlorinated. Tub temperatures vary between 103-104°.

A Wolff tanning system, massage and hair care are offered on the premises. Credit cards accepted. Phone for rates, reservations, and directions.

Portland Tub and Tan

Photos by Phil Wilcox

332   ELITE TUBBING AND TANNING

4240 SW 10th   503 641-7727
          Reservations   503 641-7735
❏   Beaverton, OR 97005

Private rent-a-tub suites in a remodeled house across from Beaverton's Montgomery Ward store. Open all year.

Private-space hot pools using chlorine-treated tap water are for rent to the public by the hour. Six indoor fiberglass hydrojet pools are maintained at a temperature of 103°. Each suite includes a shower and toilet.

Facilities include tanning equipment. Massage is available on the premises. Visa and MasterCard are accepted. Phone for rates, reservations, and directions.

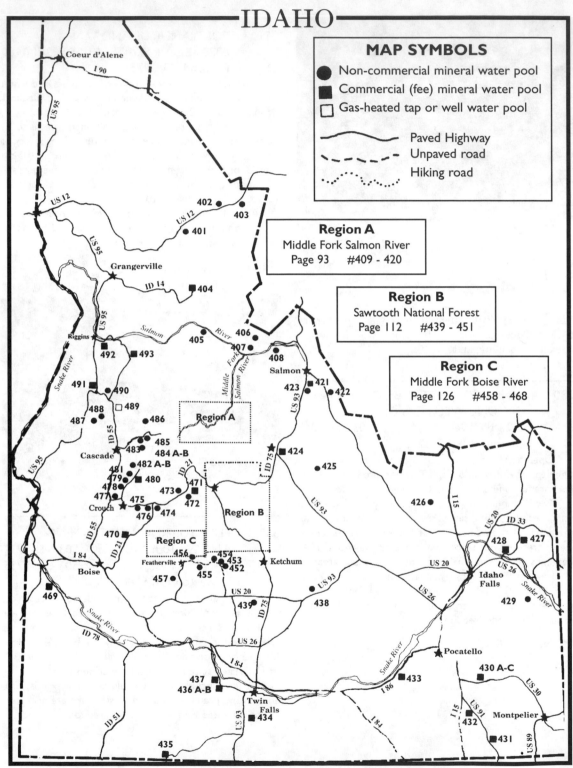

IDAHO

MAP SYMBOLS

● Non-commercial mineral water pool
■ Commercial (fee) mineral water pool
□ Gas-heated tap or well water pool

Paved Highway
Unpaved road
Hiking road

Region A
Middle Fork Salmon River
Page 93   #409 - 420

Region B
Sawtooth National Forest
Page 112   #439 - 451

Region C
Middle Fork Boise River
Page 126   #458 - 468

This map was designed to be used with a standard highway map.

Photos by Justine Hill

Directions: On US 12, drive 25 miles northeast of Lowell to the Lochsa Historical Ranger Station and Visitors Center. One mile past is the turnoff for Wilderness Gateway Campground. Go past Loops A and B and the amphitheater. Just before crossing a bridge, notice trailhead sign for Trail 211 on the left. Cross the bridge to trail parking area. Follow Trail 211 for five miles in a continuous ascent. The first half-mile is sharp, steep switchbacks. During summer months it is best to set out early in the day when most of the trail is still shaded. Five miles up when the trail forks, hikers need to follow Trail 221 to the right, descending half a mile to a flat campsite area. Cross the ingenious double-foot log bridge. When the trail forks after the bridge, turn left. This trail gently ascends for a 10- to 15-minute walk until it curves around to the right, to a large open area where the pools are located.

You may pass pack teams of horses, burros, etc. An outfitter is available near the trailhead.

Source maps: USGS *Huckleberry Butte*; *Clearwater National Forest*.

GPS: N 46.1906 W 115.1530

Stanley Hot Springs is one of the delightful hot springs possibly visited by Lewis and Clark when they traversed one of the most difficult passages through the Bitterroot Mountains and across the Continental Divide. While the Nez Perce Indians helped the explorers as much as they could, this double-footed bridge was not there to help the travelers cross the river.

401   STANLEY HOT SPRINGS

● **Northeast of the town of Lowell**

A series of delightful rock and log soaking pools in Huckleberry Creek canyon at the end of a rugged five-mile trail in the Selway-Bitterroot Wilderness. Elevation 3,600 feet. Open all year.

Natural mineral water flows out of a canyon bank at 115° and cools as it tumbles through a series of volunteer-built, log-and-rock pools that range in temperature from 90-110°. The cold creek flowing alongside offers a refreshing place to cool off. The apparent local custom is clothing optional.

There are no services available on the premises, but there are spacious campsites for backpackers and pack teams tucked into the nearby woods, where camping is permitted for up to fourteen days. There is a drive-in Forest Service fee campground at the trailhead. All other services are in Lowell, twenty-six miles west from the trailhead, or at Powell Junction, thirty-nine miles east.

402   WEIR CREEK HOT SPRINGS

● **Northeast of the town of Lowell**

Secluded, primitive hot springs and creekside soaking pool reached via a sometimes difficult rocky half-mile path in Clearwater National Forest. Elevation 2,900 feet. Open all year.

Natural mineral water flows out of several springs at 117° and down the side of the mountain where it is channeled through a wooden gutter to a large volunteer-built, eight-to-ten person, rock-bottomed pool lined with split logs. Temperature can be controlled by moving the gutter to add or divert the flow of hot water. Wooden plank benches frame the pool on three sides.

Water flows into an adjoining rock-bottomed pool at 100°. Continual flow-through keeps water in both pools fresh. From the bottom of the large pool a metal pipe carries water to a one-person pool below where it showers out at 95°. It is a short but steep, slippery, muddy walk down to this little pool just a few feet below. Fifty feet farther uphill, a small slimy-bottomed three-person rock pool has been built by volunteers over a water seepage where pool temperature is 100°. There is no flow-through and the water appears murky. The apparent local custom is clothing optional, although on a busy summer day you many encounter many families wearing swimwear.

There are no services available on the premises. It is eight miles to a Forest Service campground and twenty miles to all other services at Powell junction. Along the creek there are a few level pack-in campsites with fire pits.

Directions: From Lowell, drive 45 miles northeast on US 12 to mile marker 142. Just .1 mile past on the left, is a deep pullout on the inland side of highway, around a big curve and easy to miss. Coming from the east on US 12 from Powell, watch for mile marker 143, where a wooden bridge crosses the Lochsa River at the trailhead for Mocus Point. Go .9 miles past the bridge, look for the deep turnout on the inland side to the road. There are no signs indicating Weir Creek, only signs reminding visitors to pack out all trash, which they seem to do.

Follow the unmarked, unmaintained path on the west side of the creek for slightly less than .5 miles, staying close to the creek and not taking any spur trails heading uphill to the left. The trail climbs over rocks, fallen trees and one large boulder creekside where it seems to disappear, but it resumes on the other side of the boulder. There are muddy spots where hot water seeps up from underground, and some rock hopping is required along the creek. A series of primitive steps leads uphill to the left to the soaking pools.

Source map: *Clearwater National Forest.*
GPS: N 46.2742 W 115.0208

403　JERRY JOHNSON HOT SPRINGS

● **Southwest of the town of Missoula**

Delightful group of user-friendly, primitive hot springs at the end of an easy, one-mile hike through a beautiful forest along the east bank of Warm Springs Creek. Elevation 3,200 feet. Open all year for day use only.

Odorless natural mineral water flows out of many fissures in the creek bank at 114° and also out of several other springs at temperatures up to 110°. Volunteers have constructed rock-and-mud soaking pools along the edge of the river and near the springs. The temperature within each pool is controlled by admitting cold creek water as needed or by diverting the hotter flow to let a pool cool down. The apparent local custom is clothing optional.

There are no services on the premises and camping is not permitted near the springs. However, there are three uncrowded Forest Service campgrounds within five miles of the Jerry Johnson Hot Springs trailhead. It is ten miles to all other services at Powell Junction.

Directions: Follow US 12 to Warm Springs Park bridge trailhead, which is located .5 miles west of mile marker 152. Park in a large area on the north side of US 12, walk over the bridge and follow FS 49, which is a two-person-wide path leading one mile southeast to the springs. Where the path forks, a narrow trail to the right leads down a series of primitive steps to the creek, where hot water tumbles into several creekside rock pools. Or, continue straight on the path to an open meadow to several groups of shallow soaking pools. When coming from the west on US 12, the trailhead for the springs is 77 miles from Lowell, 170 miles from Lewiston. Coming from the east, the trailhead is approximately 22.5 miles west of Lolo Pass at the Idaho-Montana state line, 55 mile west of Lolo and 63 miles southwest of Missoula, Montana.

Source map: *Clearwater National Forest.*

GPS: N 46.2745 W 114.5224

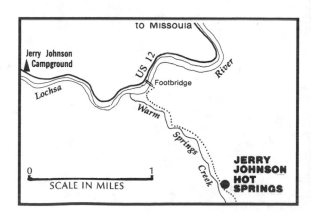

Photos by Bob Seal

404   RED RIVER HOT SPRINGS
208 842-2587
■   **Elk City, ID 83525**

Friendly, remote, rustic resort featuring both public and private-space pools surrounded by the tall timber in the Nez Perce National Forest. Elevation 4,500 feet. Open all year.

Natural mineral water flows out of ten springs at temperatures up to 130°. The chlorine-treated Olympic-size swimming pool water varies from 88° in the summer to 72° in the winter. The outdoor flow-through soaking pool is maintained at 104° and requires no chemical treatment. There are also three, claw-footed bathtubs located in private spaces. These are drained and cleaned after each use. In a fourth private space, there is an authentic galvanized horse trough that is surprisingly comfortable for a two-person soak. Two other horse troughs are also in use—one out on a side deck, and the other is placed on a hillside with a screen of trees providing almost complete privacy. Pools are available to the public as well as to registered guests. Many areas are handicap and wheelchair accessible. Bathing suits are required in public areas.

Locker rooms, a sauna, restaurant, six rustic cabins, four modern lodge units that can house from two to twelve persons, and overnight camping are available on the premises. Hiking, fishing, cross-country skiing, snowmobiling, and horse trails are nearby. It is thirty miles to a service station and 150 miles to RV hookups. Credit cards are accepted.

Directions: From the town of Grangeville, take ID 14 to Elk City, then go 25 miles east to the resort. The last 11 miles are on an easy gravel road.

405   BARTH HOT SPRINGS
●   **West of the town of North Fork**

A truly unexpected, claw-footed bathtub in a remote section of the main Salmon River known as the River of No Return. Elevation 2,700 feet. Open all year, but access is extremely difficult in the winter because the Salmon River freezes over.

Natural mineral water flows out of many small seeps at temperatures up to 140° and cools as it is gathered into a PVC pipe carrying it to the outdoor bathtub. River guides have also constructed a rock and sand soaking pool. There are no posted clothing requirements, which leaves that matter up to the mutual consent of those present.

There are no services available on the premises, nor are there any roads to this area. Access is by raft or jet boat. It is twenty-two miles to the nearest road and sixty-five miles to all services.

The Forest Service issues licenses to a limited number of outfitters who operate raft and boat trips on an individual seat and charter basis. For more information, write to Idaho Outfitters and Guides Association, Inc., Peck, Idaho, 83545.

Source maps: Forest Service, *The Salmon, River of No Return.*

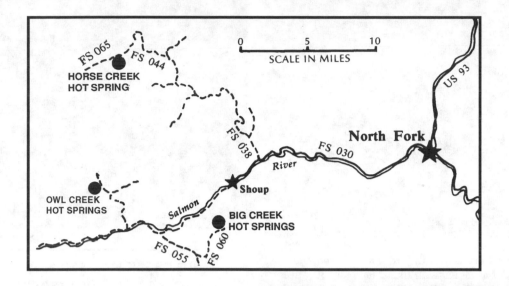

406 HORSE CREEK HOT SPRING
(see map)

● **Northwest of the town of North Fork**

Rock-lined, primitive hot spring enclosed by four walls in a very remote section of beautiful Salmon National Forest. Elevation 6,200 feet. Open during summer months, depending on snowmelt.

Natural mineral water flows out of a spring at 97° and directly into the pool, which is surrounded by a roofless bathhouse. An additional pool is down by the creek with water temperature at 99°. The apparent local custom is clothing optional.

A parking lot, rest rooms, and a picnic area with table are available near the springs. It is one-quarter mile to a campground and thirty-five miles to all other services.

Directions: From the town of North Fork, go west on FS 030 for 17 miles, turn north on FS 038 and drive 16.6 miles to FS 044. Continue west and north to FS 065 and drive 3.8 miles to the parking area at the springs. The dirt road is very winding and steep and very slippery when wet.

Source map: *Salmon National Forest*.
GPS: N 45.2328 W 114.1516

Photo by Bob Seal

Photos by Bob Seal

An old cabin sits near the creek not far from the pools. A bucket and the "fixins" for a cup of coffee are on the shelf out front. Please restock as needed and, as always, pack out your garbage.

407   OWL CREEK HOT SPRINGS
(see map on page 91)

● **West of the town of North Fork**

Soaking pools at the base of a rock cliff on the edge of Owl Creek in a remote, beautiful valley in the Salmon National Forest. Elevation 4,000 feet. Open all year; check for road closures.

Natural mineral water seeps out of the rock cliffs at temperatures ranging from 95-125° and fills two small (two person) pools, sixteen to eighteen-inches deep. The temperature can be controlled by adding cold creek water with the bucket found at the cabin. Clothing optional.

It is six miles to Ebenezer Bar campground and thirty-three miles to all other services in North Fork.

Directions: From Northfork travel 29.5 miles west on FS 030 to a small turnout on the south side of the road that holds 2-3 cars (don't block the mailboxes). The marked trailhead is 100 yards east of the turnout. The hike: Not quite 2.5 miles relatively flat trail along the east side of Owl Cree. At the 2 mile point cross the east fork of Owl Creek and continue up the west fork until you reach the cabin. Springs are located on the west side of the west fork, approximately 200 yards north of the cabin. Care should be used crossing the creek during spring and early summer due to run-off.

Source maps: *Salmon National Forest*; USGS *Bighorn Crags*.

GPS: N 45.34562 W 114.46361

Photo by Chris Andrews

408   BIG CREEK HOT SPRINGS
(see map on page 91)

● **West of the town of North Fork**

Large, waist-deep pool fed by dozens of geothermal outflows along Warm Springs Creek in a remote, rocky canyon in Salmon National Forest. Elevation 4,800 feet. Open all year.

Natural mineral water emerges from a rocky hillside at 185° and flows toward the rock and cement pool built by the Sterlings in 1987 and also through other small pools in the creekbed. Cold water is scarce, so pool temperatures must be controlled by diverting the hot water flow as needed. There is also a rock sauna at the end of a steep primitive road that may not be safe when wet. There are no services available on the premises. It is about thirty-five miles to all services in North Fork.

Directions: At North Fork turn west on FS 030 and drive 27.2 miles to FS 055. Turn left on FS 055 and drive 4 miles to FS 060. Turn left and drive another 4 miles the parking area. Walk downhill about .25 of a mile to the springs.

Source maps: *Salmon National Forest*; USGS *Shoup, Idaho-Montana*.

GPS: N 45.1829 W 114.2018

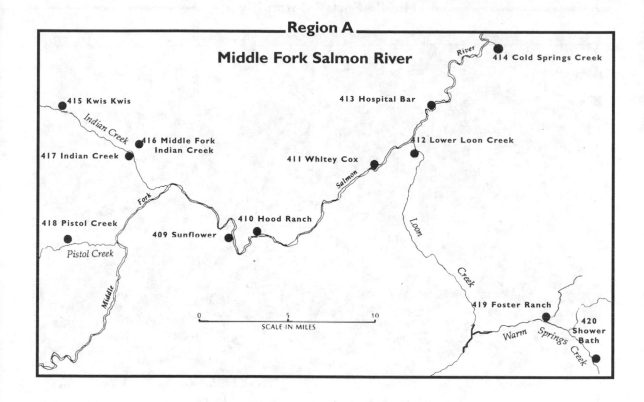

Region A

Middle Fork Salmon River

414 Cold Springs Creek

415 Kwis Kwis

413 Hospital Bar

Indian Creek

416 Middle Fork Indian Creek

412 Lower Loon Creek

417 Indian Creek

411 Whitey Cox

Fork

Salmon

410 Hood Ranch

418 Pistol Creek

409 Sunflower

Loon

Pistol Creek

Middle

Creek

419 Foster Ranch

420 Shower Bath

Warm Springs Creek

SCALE IN MILES
0   5   10

MIDDLE FORK SALMON RIVER HOT SPRINGS—BY RAFT OR TRAIL

To reach these springs, you can plan a rugged backpack route that will take you to several springs over a two- or three-day period. You can also find packaged river-raft trips, featuring hot springs on the Middle Fork of the Salmon. These tours fly you to an upriver air strip, provide rafts and all your gear, and stop at a hot springs every day.

The first step to rowing down the river, is to get to the river. This means that you and all your gear need to be flown into the area where the boats and the rest of the equipment is waiting for you.

Photos in this section by Jerry McKee

Boats pulling up to *Sunflower Flats Hot Springs*, the first stop of a five day trip.

Photo by Jayson Loam

409   SUNFLOWER FLATS HOT SPRINGS

(see map on page 93)

Natural mineral water from a group of hot springs (109°) flows through some shallow, cliff-top pools before dropping to the river's edge in the form of a hot waterfall.

410   HOOD RANCH HOT SPRINGS

(see map on page 93)

The geothermal water from springs with temperatures up to 149° cools as it flows through pipes to a crude shower-bath and soaking pool within one-hundred yards of the river.

Photo by Martin Brittan

411 WHITEY COX HOT SPRINGS
(see map on page 93)

●

A beautiful riverside meadow contains several classic, natural soaking pools supplied from nearby hot springs (131°) through channels where the water cools on the way.

412 LOWER LOON CREEK HOT SPRINGS

(see map on page 93)

●

A large, log soaking pool on the edge of Loon Creek is supplied by several springs with temperatures up to 120°. This pool does require a quarter-mile hike from the raft-landing beach where the creek joins the river.

413   HOSPITAL BAR HOT SPRINGS
(see map on page 93)

●

Dozens of fissures in rocks along the riverbank emit 115°-geothermal water that is collected for soaking in a few shallow pools next to a favorite landing spot for rafts.

414   COLD SPRINGS CREEK HOT SPRING
(see map on page 93)

●

Located a mile from the river, this spring emits 140°-mineral water that flows first into a cooling pond and then is piped to this cozy soaking box.

The ruins of Mormon Ranch are on the way up the hill to *Cold Creek Hot Spring.*

WILDERNESS HOT SPRINGS—BY TRAIL ONLY

The creeks on which these springs are located are too narrow to negotiate by raft. Walk-in trails to these springs are described in Evie Litton's book, *The Hiker's Guide to Hot Springs in the Pacific Northwest,* Falcon Press, 1998. (Their locations are marked on the map on page 93.)

415   KWIS KWIS HOT SPRINGS

●

Outflow temperature—156°

416   MIDDLE FORK INDIAN CREEK
HOT   SPRINGS

●

Outflow temperature—162°

417   INDIAN CREEK HOT SPRINGS

●

Outflow temperature—190°

418   PISTOL CREEK HOT SPRINGS

●

Outflow temperature—115°

419   FOSTER RANCH HOT SPRINGS

●

Outflow temperature—135°

420   SHOWER BATH HOT SPRINGS

●

Outflow temperature—122°

Author Evie Litton enjoying a soak at *Snively Hot Springs* in Oregon where Chris Andrews ran into her while doing research for this book.

422   SHARKEY HOT SPRING

● **East of Salmon**

A cozy wooden soaking box is all that remains of an old sheepherder's bathhouse in an open sagebrush canyon above the Lemhi Valley. Elevation 5,300 feet. Open all year.

Natural mineral water flows out of a spring at 105° directly into the four-foot by four-foot by two- foot box. The apparent local custom is clothing optional.

There are no services on the premises. It is twenty-three miles to all services.

Directions: From Salmon, drive east on ID28 to the Tendoy store. Turn left, go .2 miles and turn left again on Tendoy Lane. Drive three miles and turn right onto Warm Springs Wood Road. Follow this dirt road for two miles to the high voltage power line. Park just before crossing the bridge and walk 100 yards up a grassy trail to the spring.

Source map: *Salmon National Forest.*

GPS: N 45.01036 W 113.61196

421   SALMON HOT SPRING
RR 1 PO Box 223 B   208 756-4449
■   Salmon, ID 83467

Rustic rural plunge with a colorful past and history dating back over 100 years, currently undergoing major renovation while remaining open to the public on a day-use fee basis. Elevation 4,950 feet. Open all year.

Natural mineral water flows abundantly out of a spring 100 yards uphill at a temperature of 115° and is piped to a large outdoor recreational swimming pool that is maintained at 98° to 102°. The almost completed indoor soaking pool will be fifteen by twenty feet and maintained at 104° The flow-through pools are drained and refilled nightly, so no chemical treatment of the water is needed. Bathing suits are required although the indoor soaking pool is planned for clothing optional.

Dressing rooms and snacks are available on the premises. A lodge with rooms, additional pools, and a restaurant are nearing completion. There are several tepees for overnight rental and ample level ground for tent camping and self-contained RVs (plans for full hookups). It is eight miles to all other services in Salmon. Visa and MasterCard are accepted.

Directions: From Salmon, drive 4.5 miles south on US 93, turn left on Airport Road and drive .9 miles to a "T" intersection. Turn left again and follow Warm Springs Creek Road 3.5 miles to the spring.

Photos by Bob Seal

Sharkey Hot Spring has one of the many soaking boxes found in Idaho, that usually indicate the remains of some back-country soak for miners or cowboys.

423 GOLDBUG HOT SPRINGS

● **Southwest of the town of Salmon**

Many delightful pools and cascades of various temperatures at the end of a steep, two-mile trail up a beautiful canyon in Salmon National Forest. Elevation 5,200 feet. Open all year.

Natural mineral water flows out of several springs at temperatures up to 100° and combines with cold creek water as it tumbles down the canyon. Volunteers have added rock-and-sand dams to deepen the water-worn cascade pools. Temperatures in these cascade pools are determined by the rate of cold water runoff. Some of the pools offer a spectacular view down the canyon. The apparent local custom is clothing optional although the area is very popular and you may need to negotiate.

There are no services available on the premises. Parking is available at the trailhead, and it is one mile to all other services in Elk Bend.

Directions: On US 93 approximately 23 miles south of Salmon, look for mile marker 282. Go east on a short gravel road to the trailhead parking area. This parking lot is adjacent to private property. Cross the footbridge over Warm Springs Creek and follow the often steep trail up the canyon to the springs near the top of the ridge.

GPS: N 44.5413 W 113.5544

Upper photo by Chris Andrews
Lower photo by Bob Seal

Soakers are attracted to both the warm water and the multitudes of tropical fish that swim around.

424   CHALLIS HOT SPRINGS
H/C 63 Box 1779   208 879-4442
■   **Challis, ID 83226**

Historic pools and campground on the banks of the Salmon River. Elevation 5,000 feet. Pools open all year; campground open April 1 to November.

Natural mineral water from several springs at temperatures up to 127° flows directly into the indoor and outdoor pools that require no chemical treatment. The temperature of the outdoor pool is maintained at approximately 90°, and the temperature of the indoor pool ranges from 108-110°. Bathing suits are required.

Bed and breakfast, changing rooms, snack bar, picnic areas, camping and RV hookups (dump station) are available on the premises. It is eight miles to all other services in Challis. Major credit cards accepted.

Directions: From the intersection of US 93 and ID 75 near Challis, go southeast on US 93 and watch for signs to the hot springs.

425   BARNEY HOT SPRINGS

●   **Northeast of the town of Challis**

A large warm pond located in a remote and scenic valley (BLM land) in the middle of the high desert, with a magnificent view of two mountain ranges. Elevation 6,400 feet. Open all year; road not maintained in winter.

Natural mineral water flows into the pond from a spring at one end of the pool. The 83° water fills the very large, four-foot-deep pond. The pool is visible from the road, so bathing suits are advisable.

There are no services available on the premises. It is one-half mile to Summit Creek Campground and sixty-five miles to all other services in Challis.

Directions: From Challis, drive north on Hwy 93 for 17 miles to Ellis. Turn east toward May and Patterson on the Pahsimeroi Road. Follow this road about 25 miles past Patterson to Summit Creek Campground. The pool is .5 miles past the campground on the opposite side of the road.

Source maps: USGS *Gilmore*; *Challis National Forest* (East).

Photos by Bob Seal

Chris Andrews' favorite models are his lovely wife and daughter who often accompany him on his hot springs trips.

426   WARM SPRINGS CREEK

● **Northwest of the town of Dubois**

Two nice rock-and-sand pools in the desert foothills south of the Beaverhead Mountains, best appreciated in the hot summer as water is on the cool side. Elevation 6,400 feet. Open all year; last three and one-half miles of road not maintained year around.

Natural mineral water at 84° flows directly into two pools. The first pool is fairly shallow and large enough for two-three people. The second pool is much deeper and will hold six to eight people comfortably. Clothing optional but keep a swimsuit handy.

There are no facilities on the premises but there is a lot of level space where overnight camping is not prohibited. There is a small swimming hole located at the camping area at the 10.7 mile mark. All other services are thirty miles away in Dubois.

Directions: From Dubois (exit 167 on I 15) travel west on ID 22 17.9 miles. Turn north on a road marked "Warm Springs. Crooked Creek" and continue 7.9 miles to a fork in the road. Take the right fork towards Warm Springs Creek. Continue past several camping areas until you reach a cattleguard at 11.4 miles. Immediately past the cattleguard turn right and travel .1 mile to the fenced spring area.

Source map: USGS *Edie Ranch*.
GPS: N 44.25325 W 112.64069

Photo by Chris Andrews

Courtesy of Heise Hot Springs

427   GREEN CANYON HOT SPRINGS
■   **Box 235**   **208 458-4454**
Newdale, ID 83436

Rural, indoor plunge and RV park in a really green canyon. Elevation 6,000 feet. Open every day except Sunday from April to the end of September; open weekends the rest of the year.

Natural mineral water flows out of a spring at 118° and is piped to pools and a geothermal greenhouse. The indoor swimming pool is maintained at 96°, and the outdoor hydrojet pool is maintained at 105°. No chemical treatment is necessary. Bathing suits are required.

Locker rooms, snack bar, picnic area, streamside campground and RV hookups are available on the premises. Used extensively for family reunions and church group gatherings. It is twenty-one miles to all other services. No credit cards are accepted.

Directions: From the town of Driggs, go north and west 17 miles on ID 33. At Canyon Creek bridge, turn south and follow signs four miles to the resort.

428   HEISE HOT SPRINGS
5116 E. Heise Rd.   **208 538-7312**
800 828-3984

■   **Ririe, ID 83443**

Modernized, family-oriented resort, priding itself on home-away-from-home hospitality, with spacious, tree-shaded picnic areas and RV sites. Located on the north bank of the Snake River. Elevation 5,000 feet. Open all year; closed November.

Natural mineral water flows out of a spring at 126° and is piped to an enclosed hydrojet pool that is maintained at 105° and requires some chemical treatment. Tap water, treated with chlorine and heated by geothermal heat exchangers, is used in the other pools. An outdoor soaking pool is maintained at 92-93°, the large swimming pool at 82°, and the waterslide pick-up pool at 85°. Bathing suits are required in all areas.

Locker rooms, pizza parlor, convenience store, tackle shop, overnight camping, RV hookups, picnic area, and golf course are available on the premises. Some of the world's finest cutthroat trout fishing is nearby. It is five miles to all other services. No credit cards are accepted.

Directions: From the town of Idaho Falls, go east 22 miles on US 26 and then follow signs four miles north across the river to the resort.

Photo by Chris Andrews

429   BEAR CREEK HOT SPRINGS

●   **Southwest of the town of Palisades**

Large rock-and-sand pool near the head of a beautiful canyon in the Caribou National Forest at the end of a six to seven-mile hike. Elevation 6,350 feet. Open all year; creeks not safe to wade across during spring run-off.

Natural mineral water at 98° flows directly into a large rock-and-sand pool, over two-feet deep, capable of holding a dozen people. There are two or three other small pools to soak in at the outflow of the large pool. Clothing optional.

There are no facilities on the site, however there is plenty of open ground to camp on. It is approximately seven miles to Bear Creek campground and eleven miles to all other services in Palisades.

Directions: From the town of Palisades drive southeast on US 26 towards Alpine Way. Turn right 3.1 miles and drive across the dam. Bear left 1.6 miles later at the fork onto FS 058 (towards Bear Creek campground). Drive 5.6 miles on FS 058 and turn right into the campground. Continue .3 of a mile to the end of the road and the trail head. The hike: The trail follows the creek, crossing back and forth a few times. In most cases there is an alternate trail on the steep side hill so that crossing the creek isn't necessary. Approximately 4 miles up the trail it is necessary to cross the north fork of Bear Creek and continue up the main fork.

Proceed up the main fork for about another 1.5 miles until the trail forks. Take the left fork (Trail 148). There is a sign on this fork to Elk Mountain. The trail is quite steep for about one mile up to the top of a ridge. At the top the trail forks. The left fork is the trail to the spring. From the fork it is approximately .5 miles to the spring. You'll see unofficial camping areas off to the left just prior to the pools.

Source maps: *Caribou National Forest*; USGS *Red Ridge, Idaho* (springs not on maps).

GPS: N 43.26763 W 111.30410 (A GPS navigator comes in handy to find this spring.)

Photo by Brad Ritchie

430A   LAVA HOT SPRINGS FOUNDATION
■ **430 East Main   800 423-8597**
Lava Hot Springs, ID 83246

Two attractive and well-maintained recreation areas operated by a self-supporting state agency in the town of Lava Hot Springs. Elevation 5,000 feet.

GEOTHERMAL POOLS: (East end of town; open 363 days per year.) Natural mineral water flows out of the ground at 112° and directly up through the gravel bottoms of a Roman-style pool in a sunken garden and of a large, partly shaded soaking pool. No chemical treatment is necessary. Pool temperatures range as low as 107° at the drain end of the soaking pool. The same water is pumped to two partly shaded hydrojet pools where cold shower water may be added to control the pool temperature. Handicap accessible. Bathing suits are required. Massage is available on the premises.

SWIMMING POOLS: (West end of town; open Memorial Day to Labor Day.) Hot mineral water is piped from the geothermal springs and flows continuously through the TAC-size pool and the Olympic-size pool, maintaining a temperature of 80°. The pool complex is surrounded by a large, level lawn. Bathing suits are required.

Locker rooms are available at both locations, and it is less than three blocks to all other services. No credit cards are accepted. (See next two listings for accommodations.)

Photos by Chris Andrews

Courtesy of Riverside Inn

430C HOME HOTEL AND MOTEL
306 E. Main   **208 776-5507**
■ **Lava Hot Springs, ID 83246**

Remodeled, older hotel featuring hot mineral baths in most units, on the main street between the two Lava Hot Springs Foundation locations (see previous page). Elevation 5,400 feet. Open all year.

Natural mineral water flows out of a spring at 121° and is piped to the soaking tubs available in all rooms and in a rental house. Temperature in each tub is controllable by the customer. The eight rooms in the hotel are non-smoking; some of the sixteen rooms in the motel section permit smoking.

It is less than three blocks to a cafe, store, service station, overnight camping, and RV hookups. Visa and MasterCard are accepted.

430B RIVERSIDE INN
255 Portneuf Ave.   **208 776-5504**
Outside Idaho   **800 733-5504**
■ **Lava Hot Springs, ID 83246**

A faithfully restored historic hotel built originally in 1914, once known as the Elegant Grand Inn, picturesquely situated on the banks of the Portneuf River in an area noted for skiing, fishing, and hunting. Close to summer and winter recreation. Elevation 5,400 feet. Open all year.

Natural mineral water is pumped out of a well at 133°, then piped to two small, and one large indoor private soaking pool and one outdoor soaking pool overlooking the river where the water has now cooled down to 104°. Pools operate on a continuous flow-through basis; no chemical treatment of the water is needed. The pools are available to the public as well as to registered guests.

Sixteen nonsmoking rooms and suites, twelve with a private bath, are available on the premises. Hotel space is heated with geothermal water. All other services are within three blocks. Major credit cards are accepted. Phone for rates and information.

Courtesy of Home Hotel

431   RIVERDALE RESORT
■   **3696 N. 1600 E.**   **208 852-0266**
       Preston, ID 83263

New commercial development in a rural valley subdivision. Elevation 4,000 feet. Open all year.

Natural mineral water is pumped from a geothermal well at 112°, then piped to various outdoor pools. All soaking pools are flow-through and drained daily, eliminating the need for chemical treatment of the water. The partly shaded hydrojet pool is maintained at 103-105°, and a large soaking pool is maintained at 97-100° in the summer and 102-104° in the winter. The chlorinated junior Olympic swimming pool is maintained at 86° in the summer. A chlorinated waterslide catch pool is maintained at approximately 80°. Handicap accessible. Bathing suits are required.

A new eight-unit bed and breakfast with whirlpool tubs is a recent addition to the modern hotel rooms, all of which are non-smoking rooms. Locker rooms, snack bar, overnight camping, and RV hookups are available on the premises. It is less than six miles to a cafe, store, service station, and motel. Visa and MasterCard are accepted.

Directions: From Preston on US 91, go six miles north on ID 34 and watch for the resort signs.

Five pools of wonderful naturally warm water provide soaks, swims, and slides at *Riverdale Resort* located on Idaho's Pioneer Historic Route, Highway 34.

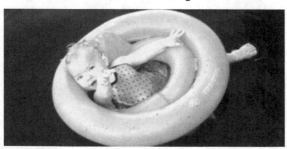

Top photo courtesy of Riverdale Resort
Other photos by Jayson Loam

Photos by Jayson Loam

Plan to stay at their bed and breakfast and enjoy all the various pools, slides, and unique tilting float located in the center of the main swimming pool.

432   DOWNATA HOT SPRINGS
25901 Downata Rd.   208 897-5736
■   **Downey, ID 83234**

Expanded, older, rural pool and picnic grounds in the rolling hills of southeastern Idaho. Elevation 4,000 feet. Pool open Memorial Day to Labor Day.

Natural mineral water flows out of a spring at 112° and is piped to outdoor pools treated with chlorine. The main swimming pool and the waterslide catch pool are maintained at 85-95°, and a hot tub is maintained at 104°. Bathing suits are required.

Bed and breakfast (open all year), pool side restaurant, catering, child care, in addition to locker rooms, snack bar, picnic grounds, overnight camping, and volleyball court are all available on the premises. After Labor Day open for private parties, water aerobics, holiday parties, and arthritis classes. Snowmobile rentals and guided tours available. It is three miles to a store, service stations, and a motel. Major credit cards are accepted.

Directions: On US 91, drive 3 miles south from the town of Downey and watch for signs.

433   INDIAN SPRINGS RESORT
3249 Indian Springs Rd.
208 226-2174
■   **American Falls, ID 83211**

Cottonwoods, willows and Russian olive trees shade the new, large hot tubs and pool in a rural Idaho setting. Elevation 5,200 feet. Open all year.

Natural mineral water flows out of a spring at 90° and Is piped to an Olympic size outdoor swimming pool that is treated with a minimum of chlorine and maintains a temperature of 90°. The pool is gravity fed and the water moves through the pool every five and one-half hours, rather than being filtered and recirculated. Two large hot tubs under the trees that can hold up to 150 people is kept at 104-106°. Some areas are handicap accessible. Bathing suits are required.

Locker rooms, picnic area, tent sites, and 125 full-hookup RV spaces are available on the premises. Cabins are in the process of being built. Call for status of construction. It is three miles to all other services. Credit cards are accepted.

Location: On Idaho Route 37, three miles south of the city of American Falls.

434   NAT-SOO-PAH HOT SPRINGS
2738 E. 2400 N.   208 655-4337
■   Hollister, ID 83301

Clean and quiet community plunge with soaking pools and acres of tree-shaded grass for picnics and overnight camping. Located on the Snake River plain, south of Twin Falls. Elevation 4,400 feet. Open May 1 to Labor Day.

Natural mineral water flows out of a spring at 99° and is piped to three outdoor pools. The swimming pool maintained at 92-94°, uses flow-through and some chlorine treatment. Part of the swimming pool flow-through is heated with a heat pump to supply the soaking pool, which is maintained at a temperature of 104-106°. The hydrojet pool, supplied by direct flow-through from the spring, maintains a temperature of 99° and requires no chemical treatment. There is also a small waterslide at the side of the swimming pool. Bathing suits are required.

Locker rooms, snack bar, picnic area, overnight camping, and RV hookups are available on the premises. It is four miles to a store and service station and 16 miles to a motel. No credit cards are accepted.

Directions: From US 93, .5 miles south of Hollister and .5 miles north of the Port of Entry, go east three miles on Nat-Soo-Pah Road directly to the location.

Photo by Phil Wilcox

435   DESERT HOT SPRINGS
208 857-2233

■   Rogerson, ID 83302

Western-style pool, bathhouse, bar, and RV park in a remote section of the Jarbridge River Canyon. Elevation 5,100 feet. Open all year.

Natural mineral water flows out of two springs at 129° into an outdoor, chlorine-treated cement tub and two indoor, flow-through soaking pools that require no chemicals. The outdoor pool is maintained at temperatures ranging from 80-90°. The two smaller, two-person tubs are maintained at 104° and 107°. Pools are open to the public in addition to registered guests. Bathing suits are required in the pool and public areas.

Dressing rooms, cafe, gas pump, cabins, overnight camping, and RV hookups are located on the premises. Horseback rides available. It is forty-nine miles to a store and service station. No credit cards are accepted.

Directions: From Twin Falls, go approximately 37 miles south on US 93. Watch for a highway sign and turn southwest .5 miles into Rogerson. At the main intersection, watch for Desert Hot Springs highway sign and follow signs 49 miles to the location. Only the last two miles are on gravel road.

Photo by Jayson Loam

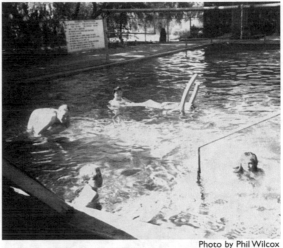

Photo by Phil Wilcox

436A BANBURY HOT SPRINGS
PO Box 348   208 543-4098
■ **Buhl, ID 83316**

Community plunge on the Snake River with soaking pools and a spacious, tree-shaded area for picnics and overnight camping. Elevation 3,000 feet. Open mid-May to Labor Day.

Natural mineral water flows out of a spring at 141° and is piped to a large, outdoor, chlorine-treated pool that is maintained at a temperature of 89-95°. Mineral water is also piped to five private-space soaking pools, some equipped with hydrojets. Water temperature in each pool is individually controlled. Each soaking pool is drained, cleaned, and refilled after each use, so that no chemical treatment of the water is needed. Bathing suits are required except in private-space pools.

Locker rooms, snack bar, overnight camping, RV hookups, and a boat ramp and dock are located on the premises. It is four miles to a restaurant and twelve miles to a store, service station, and motel. No credit cards are accepted.

Directions: From the town of Buhl, go 10 miles north on US 30. Watch for the sign and turn east 1.5 miles to the resort.

436B MIRACLE HOT SPRINGS
Route 3 Box 171   208 543-6002
■ **Buhl, ID 83316**

Remodeled health spa surrounded by rolling agricultural land. Elevation 3,000 feet. Open all year.

Natural mineral water flows out of a well at 139° and into two outdoor swimming pools, one a hotter soaking pool and the other a cooler exercise pool, and 19 roofless, enclosed soaking pools, all of which operate on a flow-through basis requiring no chemical treatment. The hotter soaking pool is maintained at temperatures from 105-110°, the cooler pool around 100°, and the temperature in the individual pools is controllable. Hydraulic lifts have been installed in the two outdoor pools. Bathing suits are required in public areas. All buildings and dressing rooms are supplied with geothermal heat.

Massage by appointment, RV hookups, and overnight camping are available on the premises. A restaurant is available within three miles, and all other services are available within ten miles. No credit cards are accepted.

Location: On US 30, ten miles north of the town of Buhl and nine miles south of the town of Hagerman.

Photo by Phil Wilcox

Photo by Chris Andrews

437 SLIGAR'S THOUSAND SPRINGS RESORT

18734 Highway 30   208 837-4987
■ **Hagerman, ID 83332**

Indoor plunge with private-space hydrojet tubs and green, shaded RV park with a view of multiple waterfalls on cliffs across the Snake River. Elevation 2,900 feet. Open all year.

Natural mineral water flows out of a spring at 200° and is piped to an indoor swimming pool, seventeen indoor hydrojet pools each large enough for eight people, and one indoor hydrojet pool large enough for twenty people. The temperature in the swimming pool is maintained between 90-96°, while the temperature in the hydrojet pools is individually controllable. All the pools are chlorinated. Bathing suits are required in public areas.

Locker rooms, boat dock, shaded picnic area, overnight camping, and RV hookups are available on the premises. A restaurant is within one mile, and all other services are within five miles. No credit cards accepted.

Location: On US 30, five miles south of the town of Hagerman.

438 WILD ROSE HOT SPRINGS

● **East of the town of Carey**

Beautiful, remote, peaceful soaking pool of crystal clear water. An abundance of wild roses near this rock-and- gravel pool give it its name. The area is surrounded by lava flows to the south and sparsely covered hills to the north. Elevation 5,000 feet. Open all year.

A natural mineral water spring flows over marshy ground at 100° to an 8 by 15-foot pool, up to three-feet deep and made of lava rock with a gravel bottom. The flow-through rate is rapid enough to eliminate most algae and leaves. The springs are located on BLM land, but the pool is on private land. Please use, but don't abuse. Bathing suits may be advisable as pool is close to the road. However, traffic is sparse and pool is not in sight—just don't stand up on the deck.

There are no services on the premises. It is fifteen and one-half miles to a campground at Craters of the Moon National Monument and thirty-four miles to all other services in Arco.

Directions: From Carey, drive 10 miles east on Highway 20-26-93. One-half mile east of mile marker 214, look for a small turnout on the north side of the road. Park and follow the trail north toward the hill. It's about 100 yards to the pool.

Map Sources: BLM *Craters of the Moon*; USGS *Paddleford Flat*.

439   MAGIC RESERVOIR HOT SPRINGS

● **East of the town of Fairfield**

A small soaking pool on the shore of Magic Reservoir near the boat ramp with views of the surrounding sage-brush-covered hills. Elevation 4,500 feet. Open all year.

Natural mineral water flows out of a spring which is located on private property. The water which comes out at 160° flows down a small channel to the shore of the reservoir into a small two-person rock-and-sand pool about one to one and one-half feet deep. The temperature in the pool usually ranges from 102-106°. The tempera-ture in the pool can be adjusted by diverting the flow of hot water or adding cold water from the reservoir. hand-icap accessible with some assistance. Bathing suits are def-initely recommended at this very public place.

There are no facilities on the premises and a store and fuel are twenty-one miles away in Fairfield.

Directions: From Fairfield drive east on US 20. Four-tenths of a mile east of mile marker 172 turn right (south) toward the Hot Springs boat landing. Continue south for .75 miles to the west edge of the parking area and walk approximately 75 yards to the spring.

Map Sources: BLM *Fairfield* (spring not on map); USGS: *Bellvue*.

GPS: N 43.32734 W 114.40001

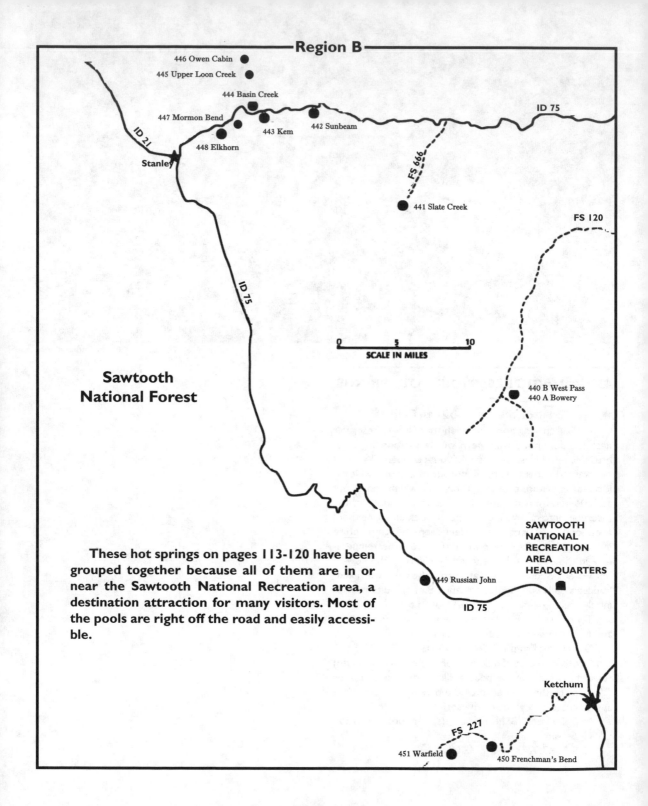

446 Owen Cabin
445 Upper Loon Creek
444 Basin Creek
447 Mormon Bend
443 Kem
442 Sunbeam
448 Elkhorn
Stanley
ID 21
ID 75
FS 666
441 Slate Creek
FS 120
ID 75
Sawtooth
National Forest
440 B West Pass
440 A Bowery
SCALE IN MILES
0 5 10
SAWTOOTH
NATIONAL
RECREATION
AREA
HEADQUARTERS
449 Russian John
ID 75
Ketchum
FS 227
451 Warfield
450 Frenchman's Bend

These hot springs on pages 113-120 have been grouped together because all of them are in or near the Sawtooth National Recreation area, a destination attraction for many visitors. Most of the pools are right off the road and easily accessible.

Photos by Bob Seal

440A   BOWERY HOT SPRING
(see map on page 112)

● **Southeast of the town of Stanley**

An outdoor bathtub and a rock-and-sand soaking pool on the edge of the South Fork of the Salmon River in the Sawtooth National Recreation Area. Elevation 6,800 feet. Road closed December 1 to May 1.

Natural mineral water flows out of a spring at 125° and through a hose to the tub and the pool. Water temperature in the tub is controlled by diverting the hot water inflow. Water temperature in the volunteer-built primitive pool is controlled by admitting cold river water. The apparent local custom is clothing optional.

There are no services on the premises. There is a walk-in campground within two miles and a drive-in campground within thirty miles. It is thirty-four miles to all other services in Clayton.

Directions: From ID 75, four miles east of Clayton, drive south on FS 120 along the East Fork of the Salmon River 28 miles to the locked gate. You will need to hike about 2 miles south down the service road toward Bowery Forest Service Station. At the bridge, follow a trail upstream 100 yards to the spring.

GPS: N 43.974 W 114.499

PRIVATE PROPERTY. NO TRESPASSING
This gate is locked because of
ENVIRO-EXTREMIST HARASSMENT
of Ranchers and Resource
Land Managers

440B   WEST PASS HOT SPRING
(see map on page 112)

● **Southeast of the town of Stanley**

A pair of out-in-the-open bathtubs along West Pass Creek, near an abandoned mine in Sawtooth National Recreation Area. Elevation 7,000 feet. Road closed December 1 to May 1.

Natural mineral water flows out of a grassy hillside at 105° and runs continuously through a hose to the ancient bathtubs, which maintain a temperature of 102°. The apparent local custom is clothing optional.

There are no services on the premises. There is a walk-in campground within two miles and a drive-in campground within thirty miles. It is thirty-four miles to all other services in Clayton.

Directions: From ID 75, four miles east of Clayton, drive south on FS 120 along the East Fork of the Salmon River 28 miles to a locked gate. Park along the fence and walk along the east side of the fence which denotes private property. (Do not go onto the private property.) You will need to walk about 1.5 miles to the abandoned mine. Hike down the trail 20 yards past the abandoned mine to the springs.

Source map: *Sawtooth National Recreation Area.*
GPS: N 43.982 W 114.486

While I am not quite sure what this sign means in general, I do know that it means that you must now take a different route (included above) to both *Bowery and West Pass Hot Springs.*

Photos by Bob Seal

Note: As of this printing the road to Slate Creek was destroyed by flash floods in September of 1998 and the springs were buried under the debris that was carried down the canyon by the rushing water. Check with the local ranger district before attempting to go to the spring.

441 SLATE CREEK HOT SPRING
(see map on page 112)

● **Southeast of the town of Stanley**

A wooden soaking box and two rock-and-sand pools in a wooded canyon in the Sawtooth National Recreation Area. Elevation 7,000 feet. Open all year.

Natural mineral water flows out of a spring at 122° and through a hose to the box, which is all that remains of a bathhouse that once stood near the HooDoo mine. Another hose brings cold water, permitting complete control of the water temperature in the box. There are also two primitive pools on the edge of the creek. The water has a slight sulphur smell. The apparent local custom is clothing optional.

There are no services available on the premises. It is seventeen miles to gas and a convenience store and thirty miles to all other services.

Directions: Drive 23 miles east of Stanley on ID 75. Turn right on FS 666 (Slate Creek Road) and drive 8.1 miles along Slate Creek to the spring.

Source map: *Sawtooth National Recreation Area*.

GPS: N 44.1017 W 114.3731

442 SUNBEAM HOT SPRINGS
(see map on page 112)

● **East of the town of Stanley**

A bathing box and several rock-and-sand pools on the edge of the Salmon River in Challis National Forest. Elevation 6,000 feet. Open all year.

Natural mineral water flows out of several springs on the north side of the road at temperatures up to 160°. The water flows under the road to several volunteer-built rock pools along the north bank of the river (upstream from the parking lot), where hot and cold water mix in a variety of temperatures; a bathing box is located downstream from the parking area. The path to the toilet and down to the springs would be wheelchair accessible requiring only three or four steps to the pools. As all pools are easily visible from the road, bathing suits are advisable.

A new toilet large enough to use as a changing room has recently been built and, except for the campgrounds, there are no other services on the premises. It is seven miles to all other services.

Location: On ID 75, at mile post 201, one mile west of Sunbeam Resort, northeast of the town of Stanley.

GPS: N 44.1600 W 114.4449

Photo by Chris Andrews

Photo by Bob Seal

443 KEM (BASIN CREEK BRIDGE) HOT SPRINGS

(see map on page 112)

● **East of the town of Stanley**

Small, primitive spring and soaking pools on the edge of the Salmon River in Sawtooth National Recreation Area. Elevation 6,000 feet. Open all year; day use only.

Natural mineral water flows out of a spring at 110° and cools as it flows through several volunteer-built, rock-and-sand soaking pools along the edge of the river. Pool temperatures may be controlled by diverting the hot water or by bringing a bucket for adding cold river water. Bathing suits are advisable in the daytime unless you check the situation out with your neighbors.

There are no services on the premises. It is seven miles to all services back towards Stanley.

Directions: On ID 75, 0.7 of a mile east of mile marker 197 look for a small parking area that will hold several cars. Park and walk down about .25 of a mile to the springs.

Source map: *Sawtooth National Recreation Area* (hot springs not shown).

GPS: N 44.26472 W 114.81208

444 BASIN CREEK CAMPGROUND HOT SPRING

(see map on page 112)

● **East of the town of Stanley**

Several shallow pools located on the edge of a creek adjacent to a campground in the Sawtooth National Recreation Area. Elevation 6,000 feet. Open all year.

Natural mineral water at 137° flows out of the ground and is mixed with cold creek water before flowing into several volunteer rock-and-sand pools. It is advisable to wear a bathing suit as the pools are near the campground.

There is an adjoining campground, and it is seven miles to all other services in Stanley.

Directions: Drive seven miles east of Stanley to Basin Creek Campground. Walk from campsite #4 through the bushes to the creek. The pools are hidden on the opposite side.

Source map: *Sawtooth National Forest* (hot springs not shown).

GPS: N 44.26447 W 114.82044

Photos by Bob Seal

445 UPPER LOON CREEK HOT SPRINGS

(see map on page 112)

● **Northeast of the town of Stanley**

A series of beautiful springs on the east side of Upper Loon Creek in the Salmon River Mountains in the beautifully wooded hills of the Frank Church Wilderness Area. Elevation 5,100 feet. Closes early and opens late, depending on snowfall.

Natural mineral water from several springs on a hillside above the creek flows at temperatures around 145° down the rock cliffs and into the pools at the edge of the creek. At the camping area there are several rock-and-sand pools that receive their hot water from slow-flowing seeps across the ground and around the next corner is a wonderful large man-made rock-and-sand pool directly beneath a waterfall. The water temperature in the pools can be adjusted by mixing in cold creek water. The apparent local custom is clothing optional.

There are no services on the premises, but there are informal spaces to pitch a tent, including one near the remains of a log cabin. The nearest campground, Tin Cup, is 6.5 miles away. It is forty miles to all other services in Stanley.

Directions: From Stanley, drive east on ID 75 13 miles to Sunbeam. Follow FS 013 north about seven miles and bear left on FS 172. Follow FS 172 over Loon Creek Summit to the Loon Creek Ranger Station. Turn right on FS 007 and follow it to the end of the road and the trailhead.

Tin Cup campground is less than a mile from the end of the road. The easy hike to the springs is about 5.5 miles each way. Look for an old cabin between the trail and the river. There are pools near the cabin, but the best ones are a few hundred yards downstream. The road is poor and not recommended for motor homes or large trailers.

Source Maps: *Challis National Forest* (West); USGS *Rock Creek.*

GPS: N 44.3835 W 114.4427

Photo by Bob Seal

Photo by Chris Andrews

446 OWEN CABIN HOT SPRING
(see map on page 112)

● **East of the town of Stanley**

Small pool in a large meadow near the ruins of the old Owen Cabin in a remote forested area noted for its cluster of hot springs. Elevation 5,200 feet. Open season depends on snow levels.

Natural mineral water flows out of the source spring at 120°, across the ground and into a small rock-and-gravel pool. The temperature in the pool depends a lot on air temperature, so test this one carefully before going in. Clothing optional.

There are no services on the premises, although there are spaces for pack-in camping. Tin Cup, the nearest campground, is eight miles away and all other services are 40 miles back in Stanley.

Directions: From Stanley, drive east on ID 75 13 miles to Sunbeam. Follow FS 013 north about seven miles and bear left on FS 172. Follow FS 172 over Loon Creek Summit to the Loon Creek Ranger Station. Turn right on FS 007 and follow it to the end of the road and the trailhead. Tin Cup campground is less than a mile from the end of the road. The easy hike to the springs is about 6 miles each way, approximately .5 of a mile past the pools at Upper Loon Creek. The road is poor and not recommended for motor homes or large trailers.

Source Maps: *Challis National Forest* (West); USGS *Rock Creek*.

GPS: N 44.3905 W 114.4409

447 MORMON BEND HOT SPRINGS
(see map on page 112)

● **East of the town of Stanley**

Small rock-and-sand pool on the south side of the Salmon River located in a scenic valley near several campgrounds and other hot springs. Elevation 5,600 feet. Accessible only during the summer when the river flow is low.

Natural mineral water flows out of a spring at 100° and fills a small, shallow rock-and-sand pool on the edge of the river. The pool needs to be rebuilt each year. Bring a suit, as pool is visible from the road.

Mormon Bend campground is on the north bank of the river and all other services are eight miles back in Stanley.

Directions: From Stanley drive east on ID 75 to mile marker 196.3 where a small, two-car turnout is located. A trail will lead to the river where you will then cross the river to the springs located near the inside corner of the river bend. You can also start the trail at the east end of the campground.

Source Maps: USGS *East Basin Creek*; *Challis National Forest* (spring not shown on either one).

GPS: N 44.26075 W 114.83867

448 ELKHORN (BOAT BOX) HOT SPRING

(see map on page 112)

● **East of the town of Stanley**

Small, wood soaking box perched on a rock between the road and the Salmon River in the Sawtooth National Recreation Area. Elevation 6,100 feet. Open all year.

Natural mineral water flows out of a spring at 136° and is piped under the road to a soaking box where the temperature is regulated by diverting the flow of hot water and pouring in buckets of cold river water. The box is too hot to get into without adding the cold water. Volunteer-built rock-and-sand pools beneath the box offer a very comfortable soak. Bathing suits are advisable as the location is visible from the road.

There are no services on the premises. It is one mile to the Salmon River Campground and two miles to all services.

Directions: On ID 75, .7 of a mile east of mile post marker 192, watch for a small turnout on the river side of the road. Head down path toward the river.

Source map: *Sawtooth National Recreation Area* (hot springs not shown).

GPS: N 44.1444 W 114.5311

Photo by Bob Seal

Photo by Phil Wilcox

While the water in the soaking box is too hot to get in without adding cold river water, by the time it flows into the pools below the box the water has cooled to a comfortable soaking temperature.

Photo by Bob Seal

Photo by Chris Andrews

Whatever the season, the pool at *Russian John* is always clear and the panoramic view is gorgeous.

449   RUSSIAN JOHN HOT SPRING
(see map on page 112)

● **North of the town of Ketchum**

Remains of an old sheepherder's soaking pool on a slope 200 yards above the highway in Sawtooth National Recreation Area. Elevation 6,900 feet. Open all year.

Natural mineral water flows out of a spring at 89° and directly into a small, clay-bottom pool that has recently been strengthened with some cement work and maintains a temperature of no more than 86°. Despite the cool temperature, this pool is so popular you may have to wait your turn. The apparent local custom is clothing optional.

There are no services available on the premises. It is eighteen miles to all services.

Directions: On ID 75, 30 yards south of mile marker 146, turn west and then south to the parking area.

Source map: *Sawtooth National Recreation Area.*

GPS: N 43.48.21 W 114.3514

Photo by Bob Seal

Photos by Chris Andrews

450   FRENCHMAN'S BEND HOT SPRING
(see map on page 112)

● West of the town of Ketchum

Several primitive roadside pools along both banks of Warm Springs Creek. Elevation 6,400 feet. Open all year for day use only.

Natural mineral water flows from the ground at more than 120° and into volunteer-built rock-and-sand pools where it is mixed with cold creek water to produce a comfortable soaking temperature. Nudity, alcohol, glass containers, non-biodegradable soap or shampoo and littering are prohibited.

There are no services on the premises. Roadside parking limitations must be observed. It is 11 miles to all services.

Directions: From ID 75 (Main Street) in Ketchum, drive 10.7 miles west on Warm Springs Road. Park in the well-marked parking area and walk 200 yards upstream to the spring.

Source Map: *Sawtooth National Recreation Area.*
GPS: N 43.3828 W 114.2926

451   WARFIELD HOT SPRING
(see map on page 112)

● West of the town of Ketchum

Natural mineral water seeps out of the earth at 119°, flows across the ground and into two rock-and-sand pools, one seven by ten-feet and the other fifteen by twenty-five feet. Temperatures in the pools range from 100-106°. A three and one-half foot concrete pool holds a temperature of about 110°. There are several more pools one hundred yards downstream. Diverting the cold water from the creek is the best way to regulate the water temperature in the pools. As the pools are at least partially visible from the road it is a good idea to keep a suit handy.

Directions: From Frenchmen's Bend parking area walk around the green gate and follow the old road about 100 yards to the springs. Two pools are on your right off the road and the others are across a bridge down by the creek and several others are further downstream.

Source Maps: *Sawtooth National Forest.* USGS: *Griffin Butte.*
GPS: N 43.63985 W 114.48724

452   WORSWICK HOT SPRINGS

● **East of the town of Featherville**

Dozens of primitive springs send a large flow of geothermal water tumbling down several acres of rolling hillside in the Sawtooth National Forest. Elevation 6,400 feet. Open all year.

Natural mineral water flows out of many springs at temperatures of more than 150°, supplying a series of volunteer-built, rock-and-log pools in the drainage channels. The water cools as it flows downhill, so the lower the pool, the lower the temperature. Most pools are quite shallow. The apparent local custom is clothing optional.

There are no services available on the premises. A campground is almost directly across FS 227. It is fourteen miles to all other services in Featherville.

Directions: From the town of Featherville, go east on FS 227 to the intersection with FS 094, then 2.2 miles farther on FS 227 and turn left after the culvert bridge to the parking area by the gate.

Source map: *Sawtooth National Forest.*

Even though this is a very popular spot, it is still possible to find a quiet place to soak in on of the pools that are off to one side.

Photo by Bob Seal

Photo by Phil Wilcox

453   PREIS HOT SPRING

● **East of the town of Featherville**

Small, two-person soaking box near the side of the road in Sawtooth National Forest. Elevation 6,000 feet. Open all year.

Natural mineral water flows out of the spring at 103° and directly into a small pool that has been given board sides and is large enough to accommodate two very friendly soakers. Bathing suits are advisable.

There are no services on the premises. It is two miles to overnight camping and fourteen miles to all other services in Featherville.

Directions: From the town of Featherville, go east on FS 227 to the intersection with FS 012, then 3.5 miles farther on FS 227. Watch for rocks surrounding the pool 10 yards from the north side of the road.

Source map: *Sawtooth National Forest.*

454   SKILLERN HOT SPRINGS

● **East of the town of Featherville**

Primitive hot springs on Big Smokey Creek, three miles by trail from Canyon Creek Campground. Elevation 5,800 feet. Open all year; trail fords the stream several times and might not be passable during high water.

Natural mineral water flows south from a spring at more than 125°, supplying a volunteer-built rock pool at the creek's edge. A few yards upstream water cascading down a rocky cliff forms a small pool for two with a comfortable temperature of 100°. Pool temperature is controllable by varying the amount of cold creek water admitted. The local custom is clothing optional.

There are no services on the premises. It is three miles to the campground and trailhead and twenty-four miles to all other services.

Directions: From Featherville, go 26 miles east on FS 227 to FS 012, turn left and immediately turn right to signed Canyon Creek Campground. Trailhead is at the north end of the campground. The trail crosses 3 small creeks before crossing unmarked Skillern Creek. The lower trail requires that you cross the very wide and cold Big Smokey Creek 3 times. The higher trail (more difficult) avoids any large creek crossing. After crossing Skillern Creek, continue about .25 of a mile and pools will be visible in the creek bed. Another, better pool is found under a ledge almost directly uphill.

Source maps: *Sawtooth National Forest*; USGS *Sydney Butte and Paradise Peak, Idaho.*

Photos by Phil Wilcox

455   BAUMGARTNER HOT SPRINGS

● **East of the town of Featherville**

Well-maintained soaking pool in popular Baumgartner Campground in Sawtooth National Forest. Elevation 5,000 feet. Open all year for day use only.

Natural mineral water flows out of a spring at 108°, supplying the soaking pool on a flow-through (no chlorine) basis and maintaining the temperature at 103°, Because of the pool's location in a campground, bathing suits are required.

Combination toilets and changing rooms are adjacent to the pool. Campground facilities are on the premises but are closed for the winter season requiring a half-mile hike into the pool. It is eleven miles to a motel, restaurant, service station and grocery store, and forty-eight miles to RV hookups.

Location: On FS 227, eleven miles east of Featherville.
Source map: *Sawtooth National Forest.*

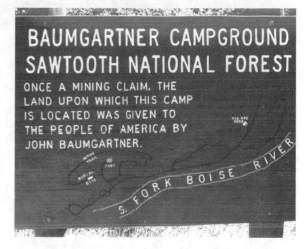

456   WILLOW CREEK HOT SPRINGS

● **East of the town of Featherville**

A series of primitive soaking pools in a lovely, small Alpine valley in the Sawtooth National Forest. Elevation 5,200 feet. Open all year.

Natural mineral water flows out of the ground at 125° and runs 100 yards across a gravel bar to join the creek. Volunteers have built an upper and lower series of rock-and-sand soaking pools where the water cools to 105° down to to 96° in the lower set of pools. The apparent local custom is clothing optional.

There is a pit toilet at the spring. There are no other services available at the spring, but there is a transfer station and corrals for equestrians at the trailhead. It is ten miles to other services in Featherville, and forty-seven miles to RV hookups.

Directions: From Featherville, drive seven miles east on FS 227 to Willow Creek, then two miles north on FS 008 to the campground and trailhead. The spring is .75 miles north on a moderate, well-maintained trail.

Source map: *Sawtooth National Forest.*

457   JOHNSON'S BRIDGE HOT SPRING

● **North of the town of Pine**

Popular series of pools at the edge of the Boise River, both at the north and south ends of the bridge. Elevation 4,400 feet. Open all year.

Natural mineral water flows out of the springs on the bank above the river. The 135° water flows through natural channels to the rock-and-sand pools at the river's edge. Several of the pools are at the north end of the bridge crossing, and there is a single pool just below the south bridge abutment. The water temperature can be controlled by mixing the hot water with cold river water, although the water swirls in and out of the pools making it impossible to maintain a single temperature. Bathing suits are required.

The springs are adjacent to Elks Flat Campground. It is four and one-half miles to gas in Pine and five miles to all other services in Featherville.

Directions: Drive 4.5 miles north of Pine to the campground and bridge.

Photos by Phil Wilcox

Middle Fork Boise River

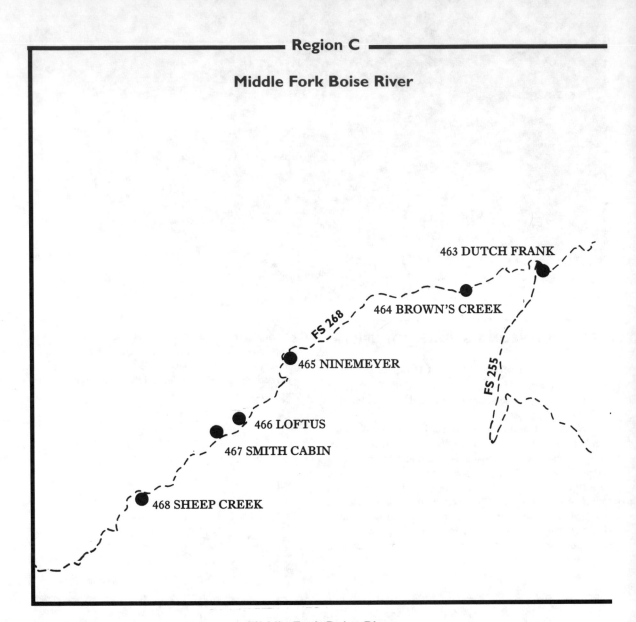

463 DUTCH FRANK

464 BROWN'S CREEK

FS 268

FS 255

465 NINEMEYER

466 LOFTUS

467 SMITH CABIN

468 SHEEP CREEK

Middle Fork Boise River
Starting Point—town of Atlanta
Pages 126–133

Some of the springs in this area are open all year, weather permitting (these are noted). Many of the pools right on the river are submerged during spring runoff and are not available until mid-July; those requiring fording the river often are not available until mid-August. The season may last until early October.

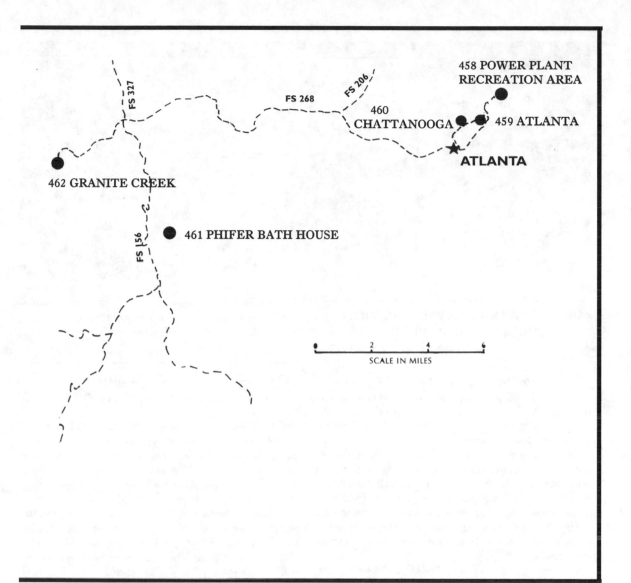

458 POWER PLANT RECREATION AREA

FS 327

FS 206

FS 268

460 **CHATTANOOGA**

459 ATLANTA

★ **ATLANTA**

462 GRANITE CREEK

FS 156

● **461 PHIFER BATH HOUSE**

2   4   6

SCALE IN MILES

Depending on which route you use to get to Atlanta, and on your type of vehicle, make sure you fill your gas tank in Boise, Idaho City, or Featherville. A store and some accommodations are available in Atlanta, but no gas. Source maps for most of the springs (some springs are not shown) are *Boise National Forest*; USGS *Atlanta East* and *Atlanta West*.

Photo by Phil Wilcox

458   POWER PLANT RECREATION AREA HOT SPRINGS
(see map on page 127)

● **Northeast of the town of Atlanta**

Several small pools adjacent to the Middle Fork of the Boise River and surrounded by wooded hillsides and open views of the Sawtooth Wilderness Area. Elevation 5,400 feet. Open all year.

Natural mineral water flows out of springs located near the river channel into several small, four- to six-foot pools, about a foot or so deep. As the pools are adjacent to the river, the water temperature can be regulated by adding river water but since the water temperature is about 100° this usually isn't necessary. The pools can be easily seen from the campground, so suits are recommended.

The pools are adjacent to Power Plant Campground, All other services are a little over a mile away in Atlanta.

Directions: Drive about 2.5 miles past Atlanta Hot Springs to the large flat "ball diamond" area at the entrance to the Power Plant Campground. The pools are located at the river's edge down a 25-foot embankment from the north end of the "ball diamond" area.

Besides the hot springs pool you might want to enjoy the "Frog Pond," a large warm swimming hole adjacent to *Atlanta Hot Springs.*

459   ATLANTA HOT SPRINGS
(see map on page 127)

● **Northeast of the town of Atlanta**

Rock-and-masonry soaking pool on a wooded plateau adjacent to a one-acre pond popular for summer swimming in the beautiful Sawtooth Mountains of Boise National Forest. Elevation 5,400 feet. Open all year; road access in winter could be difficult.

Natural mineral water flows out of a spring at 110° and cools as it travels to a nearby, volunteer-built pool, six feet by twelve feet, designed to be drained and quickly refilled after each use. The pool temperature is approximately 100°, depending on air temperature and wind conditions. The water drains into a large warm pond that locals call the "Frog Pond," which is used as a local swimming hole in the summer. This site is easily visible from the nearby road, so bathing suits are advisable.

No services are on the premises. It is one-half mile to the Power Plant Campground.

Directions: From Atlanta, follow FS 268 1.3 miles northwest. Pass a large pond on the right side of the road and park in a small turnout on the right side of the road immediately past the pond. The pool is visible from the parking area.

Photo by Bob Seal

Photo by Phil Wilcox

460   CHATTANOOGA HOT SPRINGS
(see map on page 127)

●   **Northeast of the town of Atlanta**

Large, comfortable, sand-bottom pool at the foot of a geothermal cliff surrounded by the tree-covered slopes of Boise National Forest and a magnificent view of the Sawtooth Wilderness. Elevation 5,400 feet. Open all year.

Natural mineral water flows out of fissures in a 100-foot-high cliff at 120° and cools as it tumbles toward a volunteer-built, rock-and-sand soaking pool that retains a temperature of more than 100°. The apparent local custom is clothing optional.

There are no services on the premises. It is .75 miles to Power Point Campground.

Directions: From Atlanta follow FS 268 a little over a mile northeast toward Power Plant Campground. When a large pond and Atlanta Hot Springs are visible on the right, turn left toward the river and drive to the edge of the cliff. Park and walk the cliff trail northwest for about 60 yards until you can look down and see the pool. Several well-worn, steep paths lead down about 100 feet to the pool.

Photo by Jayson Loam

Photos by Phil Wilcox

461   PHIFER BATH HOUSE
(see map on page 127)

● **West of the town of Atlanta**

A scrap wood and plastic bathhouse set in the rugged mountains on the Middle Fork Boise River. Elevation 4,400 feet. Open all year; road access in winter could be difficult.

Natural mineral water flows out of a warm artesian well at 85° and is piped from the wellhead to the bath house that has a shower stall and tub. The apparent local custom is clothing optional.

It is eight miles to Queen's River Campground although many people camp along Phifer Creek.

Directions: Drive 17 miles west of Atlanta on FS 268 to the intersection of FS 327 and FS 156. Follow FS 156 south over the bridge, crossing the Middle Fork Boise River and immediately turn left on the first road. The short .25 mile road fords Phifer Creek and ends at the bathhouse. The ford is often washed out so just walk the quarter mile.

462   GRANITE CREEK HOT SPRING
(see map on page 127)

● **West of the town of Atlanta**

Large, deep pool located between FS 268 and the Middle Fork Boise River surrounded by wooded hills and considered by some to be one of the best. Elevation 4,200 feet. Open seasonally.

Natural mineral water flows out of several springs with temperatures up to 130° and runs through channels to a 12-foot by 20-foot, waist-deep, rock-and-sand pool located on the river's edge. Cold water from the river can be added to the pool to control the temperature. The pools are close to the road, so suits are advisable.

There are no services on the premises, and it is eleven miles to Idaho Outdoor Association Campground.

Directions: Drive 3.5 miles west on FS 268 from the intersection of FS 237 and FS 156. Continue about 3.5 miles and look for a large parking area cut into the hill on the right. The pool is easily visible from the road.

Photos by Phil Wilcox

463 DUTCH FRANK (ROARING RIVER) HOT SPRINGS
(see map on page 126)

● **Southwest of the town of Atlanta**

Several small pools at the bottom of a canyon on the edge of the Middle Fork Boise River. Elevation 4,100 feet. Open seasonally.

Natural mineral water flows from many small springs along several hundred yards of shoreline at temperatures up to 150°. Natural channels disperse the water into several small rock-and-sand pools that can be mixed with river water to adjust the hot water temperatures which range from 103-120°. As the river level lowers it might be necessary to dig out some new pools. Pools are highly visible from the road, and swimsuits are advisable.

There are no services on the premises and it is ten miles to Ninemeyer Campground.

Directions: Drive west from Atlanta on FS 268 for 22 miles to the junction of FS 255 at Roaring River. Turn south and cross the Middle Fork Boise River on FS 255 to a small parking area. Walk a hundred yards east to the highly visible thermal area.

464 BROWN'S CREEK HOT SPRING
(see map on page 126)

● **Southwest of the town of Atlanta**

Gorgeous photo-opportunity hot water shower on the opposite bank of the Middle Fork Boise River in a narrow canyon with steep hills and very fast water. This one is tricky to get to even at low water in late summer. Elevation 3,900 feet. Open seasonally.

Natural mineral water cascades from springs on a cliff above the pool at 120°, cooling as it flows down the cliff into a small six- by six-foot soaking pool at the base of the shower. The pool is easily visible from the road, and bathing suits are advised.

It is seven miles to the Ninemeyer Campground.

Directions: From Atlanta, drive 25 miles west on FS 268 look for hot water flowing down the cliff on the south side of the river. Parking is available in a turnoff directly opposite the spring. The river is swift at this point and caution should be used when fording the river.

Photo by Bob Seal

Photo by Bob Seal

Next to the hot pool volunteers have built a large, deep swimming hole.

465   NINEMEYER HOT SPRINGS
(see map on page 126)

● **Southwest of the town of Atlanta**

Small pools on the south side of the Middle Fork Boise River across from a campground with a wonderful adjacent swimming hole. Elevation 3,700 feet. Open seasonally (late August to October).

Several springs at 169° flow gently down the hillside to a riverside rock-and-sand pool that is presently about six by eight feet. The pool can be cooled by adding river water. It is easily visible from the road, and bathing suits are advised.

The springs are at Ninemeyer Campground.

Directions: From Atlanta drive west on FS 268 about 30 miles to Ninemeyer Campground. Look for the steamy hillside and pools directly across the river from the campground.

Source Map: USGS *Barber Flats*.

466   LOFTUS HOT SPRINGS
(see map on page 126)

● **Southwest of the town of Atlanta**

One of the more romantic spots with a warm shower, peaceful pools, and a grotto-like overhang lending a sense of privacy. Located above the road with a lovely view of the river and surrounding woods. Elevation 3,600 feet. Open all year.

Natural mineral water at 130° showers over the edge of an overhang into an eight-foot, very clean, sandy-bottom pool. The water in the upper pool, now at 105°, continues to flow into a lower six-foot pool supplied by the main pool runoff. The apparent local custom is clothing optional or by common consent.

Be aware: there is a great deal of poison oak, so watch where you put your towel.

It is four miles to Ninemeyer Campground.

Directions: From Atlanta, drive 34 miles west on FS 268. Look for a turnoff to the north and hot water flowing down the hill. The pools are a few yards up the hill from the parking area.

Photo by Phil Wilcox

Photos by Phil Wilcox

467 SMITH CABIN HOT SPRINGS
(see map on page 126)

● **Southwest of the town of Atlanta**

Small rock pools on both sides of the Middle Fork Boise River. Elevation 3,500 feet. Open seasonally.

Natural mineral water flows out of the hillside above the river on the north bank and into volunteer-built, rock-and-sand pools on a gravel bar at the river's edge. On the south side, water flows to a small, shallow pool at the river's edge. These pools can only be accessed when the river is slow (mid-August) and are visible upstream from the ones on the north side. The hot water temperature of 138° can be controlled by adding river water. Bathing suits are advisable.

It is one-half mile to Troutdale Campground.

Directions: From Atlanta, drive west on FS 268 for about 35 miles. Look for a small rock pool on the near side of the river .7 miles after crossing a bridge over the river. Parking turnout is not available, but the road is wide here and traffic light.

Map Source: USGS *Sheep Creek* (pools on north side only).

468 SHEEP CREEK BRIDGE HOT SPRINGS
(see map on page 126)

● **Southwest of the town of Atlanta**

Shallow rock pool dug into a hillside several feet above the Middle Fork Boise River. Elevation 3,400 feet. Open all year.

Natural mineral water flows in a weak trickle down the hillside to a shallow rock pool laden with algae. The 142°-water cools as it flows down the hillside, and air contributes to the rest of the cooling. Bathing suits advised.

It is two and one-half miles to Troutdale Campground.

Directions: From Atlanta, travel 38 miles to a bridge where the road recrosses the river. Park in a small turnout at the east end of the bridge. The spring is located several feet above the river, 50 yards downstream from the bridge.

469 GIVENS HOT SPRINGS
HC79 Box 103 208 495-2000
■ **Melba, ID 83641**

Rural plunge, picnic grounds, and RV park on agricultural plateau above the Snake River. Elevation 3,000 feet. Open all year.

Natural mineral water flows out of an artesian spring at 120° and is piped to a minimally chlorine-treated, indoor swimming pool and six indoor, private-space soaking pools that operate on a drain-and-fill basis. The swimming pool is maintained at a temperature of 92-93° in the winter and 99-100° in the summer. The temperature in the tubs is individually controllable, with temperatures ranging from 105-110°. Bathing suits are required.

Dressing rooms, suit and towel rentals, two cabins, snack bar, picnic grounds, softball diamond, volleyball, horseshoes, fishing on the Snake River, RV hookups, and overnight camping are available on the premises. Facilities available for family reunions. It is three miles to a boat dock, and eleven miles to all other services in Marsing. No credit cards are accepted.

Location: Eleven miles southeast of the town of Marsing on ID 78.

Photo by Jayson Loam

Warm Springs Resort began by providing laundry services, baths and swimming to the Boise Basin Gold Rush miners and early pioneers. It also served as an overnight stage stop, and a hospital in the late 1800s.

Courtesy of Givens Hot Springs

470 WARM SPRINGS RESORT
PO Box 28 208 392-4437
■ **Idaho City, ID 86361**

Scenic and historic ride from Boise brings you to these rural pools and RV park surrounded by the Boise National Forest. Elevation 4,000 feet. Open all year; days and hours vary with the seasons.

Natural mineral water flows out of a spring at 110° and through an outdoor swimming pool maintained at a temperature of 94° in summer and 97° in winter. Chemical treatment of the water is minimal. The pool is open to the public as well as to registered guests. Bathing suits are required.

Heated dressing rooms, suit and towel rentals, snack bar, cabins, overnight camping, and RV hookups are available on the premises. Seasonal outdoor sports in the immediate area. Group facilities for reunions, parties, etc. A cafe, store, and service station are located within two miles. Credit cards are accepted.

Location: On ID 21, one and one-half miles south of Idaho City, recently rebuilt as a colorful mining town, and thirty-seven interesting miles from Boise.

472 SACAJAWEA HOT SPRINGS

● **West of the town of Grandjean**

Popular, large geothermal area on the north bank of the South Fork of the Payette River in Boise National Forest. Elevation 5,000 feet. Open all year.

Natural mineral water flows out of many springs at temperatures up to 108° and cools as it cascades into a series of volunteer-built rock pools along the river's edge. Because the pools are visible from the road, bathing suits are advisable.

There are no services available on the premises. It is one mile to a cafe, cabins, overnight camping, and RV hookups at Sawtooth Lodge, and forty miles to a store and service station in Stanley.

Directions: From Lowman, drive 21 miles east on ID 21 to Grandjean turnoff (FS 524) on the right. Follow the gravel road 4.6 miles to Wapiti Creek Bridge. Look for springs on the right side of read, .6 miles past the bridge.

GPS: N 44.0940 W 115.1848

471 SAWTOOTH LODGE
130 N. Haines   208 259-3331
■ **Grandjean, ID 83712**

Historic mountain resort in the Sawtooth Recreation Area two blocks from the South Fork Payette River. Elevation 5,100. Pool open Memorial Day through Labor Day; resort remains open through October.

Natural mineral water flows out of several springs with temperatures up to 150° and into an outdoor, chlorinated swimming pool maintained at approximately 80°. The pool is available to the public as well as to registered guests. Bathing suits are required.

Dressing rooms, restaurant serving mountain-style home cooking, log cabins, overnight camping, and RV hookups are available on the premises. Horses, trail rides, pack trips, hunting, fishing, hiking all located nearby. It is forty-two miles to a store and service station in Stanley. Visa and MasterCard are accepted.

Directions: From the town of Lowman, go 22 miles east on ID 21, then follow signs six miles on gravel road to the lodge, one mile past Sacajawea Hot Springs.

Photos by Bob Seal

Photos by Phil Wilcox

474   KIRKHAM HOT SPRINGS

● **East of the town of Lowman**

Popular geothermal area with many hot waterfalls and pools adjoining a National Forest campground on the South Fork of the Payette River. Elevation 4,200 feet. Open all year.

Natural mineral water flows out of many springs and fissures along the south bank of the river at temperatures up to 120° and cools as it cascades toward the river. Volunteers have built several rock-and-sand soaking pools in which temperatures can vary above or below 100° depending on air temperature and wind conditions. Bathing suits are advisable, especially in the daytime.

Overnight camping is available in the adjoining campground. It is thirty-eight miles to a cafe, store, service station, and cabins and thirty-four miles to RV hookups, all located near Stanley.

Directions: From the town of Lowman, go four miles east on ID 21 and watch for the Kirkham Hot Springs Campground sign.

Source map: *Boise National Forest.*

GPS: N 44.0421 W 115.3241

473   BONNEVILLE HOT SPRINGS

● **West of the town of Grandjean**

Popular, semi-remote area on a tree-lined creek in Boise National Forest. Elevation 4,800 feet. Open all year.

Natural mineral water flows out of a multitude of springs with various temperatures up to 180°. Be careful not to step into any of the scalding runoff channels. There is one small, wooden bathhouse with an individual tub supplied with water from a nearby spring at a temperature of 103° and a cold water pipe to help cool the water. Soakers drain the tub after each use. There are also many volunteer-built, rock-and-sand soaking pools along the edge of the creek where the geothermal water can be mixed with cold water. Bathing suits are optional based on the desire of those present.

An adjacent campground with toilets is available for a fee. It is eight miles to a cafe, cabins, and RV hookups and forty miles to a store and service station in Stanley.

Directions: From Lowman, on SR 21, drive 19 miles northeast to Bonneville Campground (formerly Warm Springs Campground). From the north edge of the campground, follow the unmarked but well-worn path .25 miles to the geothermal area.

GPS: N 44.0924 W 115.1848

> There is now a charge to park while using the pools. However, if you camp at Bonneville, Kirkham, or Pine Flats, the host will give you a pass that allows you to park free at any of the three locations.

475   PINE FLATS HOT SPRING

● **West of the town of Lowman**

Spectacular, geothermal cascade and cliffside soaking pool overlooking the South Fork of the Payette River in Boise National Forest. Elevation 4,100 feet. Open all year.

Natural mineral water with temperatures up to 125° flows from several springs on top of a 100-foot-high cliff, cooling as it spills and tumbles over the rocks. There is one volunteer-built, tarp-lined rock pool thirty feet above the river, immediately below a hot shower-bath that averages 104°. Other rock pools at the foot of the cliff have lower temperatures. The apparent local custom is clothing optional.

The hot springs are located one-third of a mile from the Pine Flats Campground and parking area. It is thirty-eight miles to a cafe, store, service station, and motel and twenty-seven miles to RV hookups, all near the town of Stanley.

Directions: From the west edge of Pine Flats campground, on SR 21 driving from Crouch toward Lowman, follow an unmarked but well-worn path .33 miles west down to and along a large riverbed and rock-and-sand bar. Look for geothermal water cascading down the cliff onto the bar.

Source map: *Boise National Forest.*
GPS: N 44.0306 W 115.4117

A short walk from the campground puts your feet in a warm-water runoff and the lower pools. An easy climb takes you up to the wonderful water fall and deeper hot pool near the top of the cliffs.

Photo by Phil Wilcox

476   HOT SPRINGS CAMPGROUND

● **East of the town of Crouch**

The cement foundations of a long-gone bathhouse and some small, volunteer-built soaking pools are intended to use some of the continuing hot-water flow. Located on a riverbank across the highway from a National Forest campground. Elevation 3,800 feet. Open all year.

Natural mineral water flows out of several springs at 105° and into volunteer-built, shallow, rock-and-sand pools near the south side of the highway. Bathing suits are advisable.

Overnight camping is available on the premises. All other services are available four miles away in Crouch.

Directions: From the town of Crouch, go four miles east toward Lowman. Look for Hot Springs Campground one mile after entering Forest Service land.

Source map: *Boise National Forest.*

477   DEER CREEK HOT SPRINGS

● **West of the town of Crouch**

Small, volunteer-built soaking pool less than ten yards from a paved highway, combining the flow from several springs, a test well, and a creek. Elevation 3,000 feet. Open all year.

Natural mineral water flows out of multiple springs and an abandoned well casing at temperatures ranging up to 176°. Volunteers have built a shallow, plastic-and-sand soaking pool on the river side of the South Fork Payette River where you can mix the hot and cold water to achieve a pleasant temperature. There are no posted clothing requirements, but the proximity to the highway makes bathing suits advisable.

There are no services available on the premises, but all services are available four miles away in Crouch.

Directions: From the town of Crouch, go 4.5 miles west toward the town of Banks. From Banks, on Hwy 55, got to mile post 4 on the Crouch-Lowman Highway. There is a good pull-out area next to the river. (Do not go onto the steep dirt road on the north side of the highway; it dead ends in just a few yards. Park in the turnout and walk back to the springs which are just below the steep side road.

Source map: *Boise National Forest.*
GPS: N 44.09014 W 116.05168

Photos by Phil Wilcox

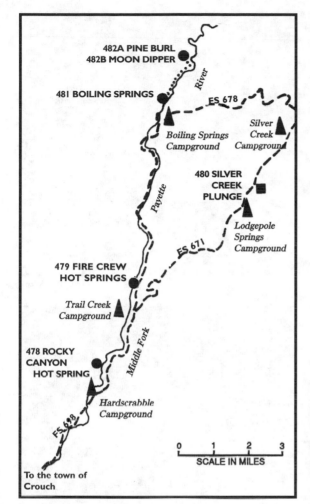

To the town of Crouch

478   ROCKY CANYON HOT SPRING
(see map)

● **North of the town of Crouch**

Primitive hot spring across the river on the Middle Fork of the Payette in Boise National Forest. Elevation 4,000 feet. Open all year.

Natural mineral water flows out of a spring at 120°, then down a steep slope toward the river. To reach the spring, you must ford the river, which might not be safe during high water. Volunteers have built a series of primitive rock pools, each colder than the one above. All pools are visible from the road, so bathing suits are advisable.

There are no services available on the premises. It is one and one-half miles to Hardscrabble Campground, and ten miles to all other services in Crouch.

Directions: From Crouch, take FS 698 about 12.5 miles and park in a turnout on your left. Pools are across the river, and fording the river should only be done in late summer or early fall.

Source map: *Boise National Forest.*
GPS: N 44.25190 W 115.89082

Photo by Chris Andrews

Photo by Phil Wilcox

479 FIRE CREW HOT SPRINGS
(see map on page 139)

● **North of the town of Crouch**

Several pools in a winding river canyon at the edge of the Middle Fork of the Payette River in Boise National Forest. Elevation 3,800 feet. Open all year.

Natural mineral water flows from springs at temperatures above 120° into a fifteen-foot, rock-edged pool adjacent to the river. By moving the rocks, cold river water can be added to the pool to adjust the temperature. If the river water is too low to let in cold water be very careful getting into the soaking pool as the water may be extremely hot. The apparent local custom is clothing optional.

It is one-half mile to Trail Creek Campground and fifteen miles to Crouch for all other services.

Directions: From Crouch, drive north on FS 698 toward Boiling Springs. About .3 miles past the junction with FS 671, look for a dirt road, #698L8, on the river side of FS 698. Follow the road for a short distance to a turn-around and parking area. The pools are located on the upstream end of the parking area. The road is not recommended for RVs or trailers. If you decide to walk in, it is only about .25 of a mile.

GPS: N 44.28186 W 115.87400

Photo by Chris Andrews

Courtesy of Silver Creek Plunge

480   SILVER CREEK PLUNGE
2345 Silver Creek Rd   208 870-0586
(see map on page 139)
■   **Garden Valley, ID 83622**

Remote, mountain resort surrounded by Boise National Forest. Elevation 4,700 feet. Operated partially on National Forest Systems Lands. Open all year; snowmobile access in winter.

Natural mineral water flows out of a spring at 101° directly into an outdoor swimming pool that is maintained at 95°. The pool operates on a flow-through basis, requiring a minimum of chlorination. It is available to the public as well as to registered guests. Bathing suits are required.

Dressing rooms, convenience store, snack bar, cabins (with advance reservations), and overnight camping are available on the premises. It is twenty-two miles to a service station, and RV hookups. Electricity is generated on a limited basis. During snowy weather the owners provide a sno-cat shuttle service from about one mile after the pavement stops to the resort. Credit cards are accepted.

Directions: From the town of Crouch, go north 14 miles on FS 698 (Middle Fork Road), then bear northeast on FS 671 for 9 miles to the plunge. Follow the signs.

Source map: *Boise National Forest.*

Photo by Phil Wilcox

Heavy snow doesn't need to deter your visit to *Silver Creek Plunge*—they have a brand new sno-cat that will come and get you.

481   BOILING SPRINGS
(see map on page 139)

● **North of the town of Crouch**

Large, geothermal water flow on the Middle Fork of the Payette River in Boise National Forest. Elevation 4,200 feet. Open all year.

Natural mineral water flows out of a cliff at more than 130° into a pond adjacent to the Boiling Springs guard station. The water cools as it flows through a ditch to join the river. Summer volunteers usually build a rock-and-mud dam at the point where the water is cool enough for soaking or where river water can be added. The best pool to soak in is the one under the overhang, at 108°, as the riverside pools are usually quite shallow. Because of the nearby campground, bathing suits are advisable.

No services are available on the premises. It is one-quarter of a mile to Boiling Springs Campground and nineteen miles to all other services in Crouch.

Directions: From the north edge of Boiling Springs Campground, follow the path .25 miles to the rental cabin (which used to be the guard station) and the spring. You might also like to visit Moon Dipper and Pine Burl Hot Springs which are on the same trail.

Source map: *Boise National Forest.*
GPS: N 44.36353 W 115.74983

Photos by Phil Wilcox

482A MOON DIPPER HOT SPRING AND
482B PINE BURL HOT SPRING
(see map on page 139)

● **North of the town of Crouch**

Two lovely, remote and primitive hot springs on the bank of Dash Creek, very close together in Boise National Forest. Elevation 4,200 feet. Open all year.

Natural mineral water flows out of the cliff face at 130° and directly into volunteer-built, rock soaking pools. Water temperature in the pools is controlled by mixing cold creek water with the hot water. Moon Dipper, a large, sandy-bottom pool, has a nice canyon view, while Pine Burl offers a small, romantic spot for two. The apparent local custom is clothing optional.

No services are available on the premises. It is a two-mile hike to overnight camping and twenty-one miles to all other services.

Note: There are several more primitive hot springs with the potential for volunteer-built soaking pools further upstream from Moon Dipper and Pine Burl. However, all of them require that the river be forded many times with a high risk of losing the faint, unmarked path. Consult a Boise National Forest ranger before attempting to hike to any of these springs.

Directions: From the former Boiling Springs guard station (now a rental cabin) on the hillside, follow a well-used (sometimes slippery), moderately easy, unmarked trail for a two-mile hike to the springs. Just after passing a hot water source on your left (too hot), and a nice sandy beach on your right you will come to Dash Creek. Go left up the creek for a few yards and Moon Dipper will appear. Pine Burl is a few more yards up Dash Creek.

Source maps: *Boise National Forest*; USGS *Boiling Springs, Idaho* (springs not on quad).

Photos by Phil Wilcox

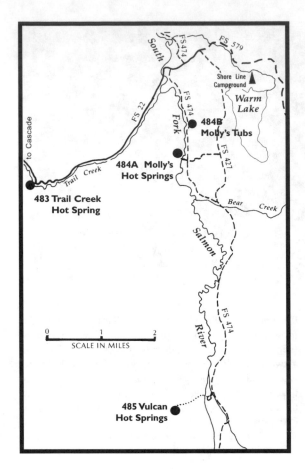

483   TRAIL CREEK HOT SPRING
(see map)

● **West of Warm Lake**

Small, beautiful hot spring, soaking pool in a narrow canyon down a steep sixty-yard path from a paved highway in Boise National Forest. Elevation 6,000 feet. Open all year.

Natural mineral water flows out of a fissure in the rocks adjoining Trail Creek at 125°. (Reports are that volunteers have placed a hot tub in the creekbed to replace the old bathtub and installed a hose to bring in the hot water.) Bring a bucket with which to add cold creek water when desired. Volunteers have also built a primitive, rock-and-sand soaking pool on the edge of the creek where the temperature can be controlled by changing the amount of cold creek water admitted. You may have to rebuild this pool if you are the first ones in, as high water tends to wash it out every year. The apparent local custom is clothing optional.

No services are available on the premises. It is two miles to a campground, seven miles to gas, cafe, cabins, and phone at Warm Lake Lodge (open Memorial Day to October 15), and twenty-two miles to all other services in Cascade.

Directions: from the intersection of FS 22 and FS 474 west of Warm Lake, go west 3.7 miles and look for an especially large parking area on the south side of the road. From the west edge of this parking area, the pool is visible at the bottom of Trail Creek canyon. There is no maintained trail, so be careful scrambling down the steep path.

Source map: *Boise National Forest.*
GPS: N 44.62554 W 115.74983

At the time Bob Seal took this photo the new tub at *Trail Creek* had not been hooked up yet.

484A   MOLLY'S TUBS
(see map on page 144)

● **West of Warm Lake**

A much-used collection of bathtubs on the South Fork of the Salmon River in Boise National Forest. Elevation 5,200 feet. Open all year.

Natural mineral water flows out of several springs at approximately 136° and is piped through hoses to eight bathtubs. Buckets are used for adding cold water from the nearby river. The tubs are lined up in two groups so you can have relative privacy if desired. Buckets and rubber stoppers for the tubs were there at last report. There are also pools at the river's edge that are rebuilt each year after the high water level recedes. The apparent local custom is clothing optional.

There are no services available on the premises. It is one and one-half miles to Shoreline campground, three and one-half miles to Warm Lake Lodge (open Memorial Day to October 15), and twenty-four miles to all other services in Cascade.

Directions: From the intersection of FS 22 (paved) and FS 474 (gravel), go 1.3 miles south on FS 474 to a pull-out on right. Follow a steep path down to the tubs.

Source map: *Boise National Forest.*
GPS: N 44.3828 W 115.4143

484B   MOLLY'S HOT SPRING
(see map on page 144)

● **West of Warm Lake**

A sandy-bottom pool on the side of a steep, geothermal hillside overlooking the South Fork of the Salmon River in Boise National Forest. Locals named this one "the Duke" in honor of repeated visits from John Wayne and Robert Mitchum. Elevation 5,400 feet. Open all year.

Natural mineral water flows out of several springs at temperatures up to 120° and is transported downhill by a variety of pipes and hoses. Water temperature in the volunteer-built pool is controlled by diverting or combining the hotter and cooler flows. Additional volunteer work could produce an excellent chest-deep pool. The apparent local custom is clothing optional.

No services are available on the premises. It is two miles to overnight camping at shoreline, four miles to gas, cafe, store, cabins, and phone at Warm Lake Lodge (open Memorial Day to October 15), and twenty-five miles to all other services in Cascade.

Directions: From the intersection of FS 22 (paved) and FS 474 (a signed gravel road to Stole Meadows), go 1.9 miles south on FS 474 to the intersection with a road where a sign directs you east to Warm Lake. The road leading west from this intersection has been blocked to vehicle traffic, but it is passable on foot. Park and walk west on this blocked road 300 yards, cross the old bridge, and immediately turn right onto a trail that is just above the fallen trees at the waters edge. Follow the trail 100 yards north to the thermal area. This spring is .4 of a mile further than Molly's Tubs.

Source map: *Boise National Forest.*
GPS: N 44.3829 W 115.4143

Photos by Phil Wilcox

485 VULCAN HOT SPRINGS
(see map on page 144)

● **South of Warm Lake**

Still popular, geothermal creek pools in the Boise National Forest which seem to be getting hotter each year. The pools are considered by many to be too hot to even bother with. The trees, once insect-ravaged, seem to be making a comeback. Elevation 5,600 feet. Open all year.

Natural mineral water flows out of many small, bubbling springs at boiling temperatures (138° in places), creating a substantial hot creek that gradually cools as it runs through the woods toward the South Fork of the Salmon River. Volunteers had built a log dam across this creek at a point where the water had cooled somewhat. This dam has been partly wiped out by high-water runoff, and the one-mile trail to the springs is no longer maintained. The apparent local custom is clothing optional.

One mile south of Stole Meadows there is an unmarked, unofficial camping area where the trail head to the springs begins. It is seven miles to a Forest Service campground and thirty-two miles to all other services.

Directions: At the west edge of the camping area is a log footbridge built by the Corps of Engineers. Cross this bridge and follow the path across two more log bridges. It is approximately one mile to the dam and pool.

Source maps: *Boise National Forest*; USGS *Warm Lake, Idaho*.

Photo by Bob Seal

Photo by Chris Andrews

486 SUGAH (MILE 16) HOT SPRING

● **North of Warm Lake**

A sweetie of a remote soaking pool for two, located on the edge of the South Fork of the Salmon River in Payette National Forest. Elevation 4,800 feet. Open all year.

Natural mineral water flows out of a spring at 115° and cools as it goes through a makeshift pipe to the beautifully constructed rock-and-masonry pool at the river's edge. Pool temperature is controlled by diverting the hot water and/or by adding a bucket of cold river water. The apparent local custom is clothing optional.

There are no services available on the premises. There is a campground within two miles, and it is forty miles to all other services.

Directions: From the intersection of FS 22 (paved) and FS 474, go north on FS 474 along the South Fork of the Salmon River for 16 miles to the spring. At 1.6 miles past Poverty Flats Campground, there is a small (two-car) turnout on the side of the road toward the river. Look for an unmarked, steep path down to the pool.

Source maps: *Payette National Forest; Boise National Forest.*

GPS: N 44.84685 W 115.69707

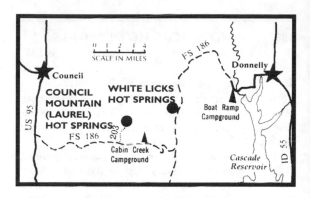

487   COUNCIL MOUNTAIN (LAUREL) HOT SPRINGS

(see map)

● **East of the town of Council**

Several primitive, thermal springs in a wooded canyon at the end of a rugged, two-mile hike in the Payette National Forest. Elevation 4,300 feet. Open all year.

Natural mineral water flows out of several springs at temperatures up to 120° and into progressively cooler, volunteer-built soaking pools along the bottom of Warm Springs Creek. Clothing optional.

There are no services on the premises. It is two miles to Cabin creek Campground and twenty-three miles to all other services in Council.

Directions: From Cabin Creek Campground on FS 186 go 1.8 miles west to the trailhead at milepost 9. Follow trail number 203 two miles north to the springs being very careful when the trail crosses the creek as the water is often very hot.

GPS: N 44.66891 W 116.30563

To the people around the the town of Council, this wonderful place to soak is known simply as "the springs."

Photos by Chris Andrews

Photo by Chris Andrews

● **West of the town of Donnelly**

A large, geothermal seep serving two small bathhouses in an unofficial camping area at a wooded site surrounded by Payette National Forest. Elevation 4,800 feet. Open all year.

Natural mineral water flows out of many small springs at temperatures up to 120°, supplying two small, wood shacks, each containing a cement tub. Each tub is served by two pipes, one bringing in 110° water, the other bringing in 80° water. The tub temperature is controlled by plugging up the pipe bringing in the water not desired. Soakers are expected to drain the tub after each use. Bathing suits are not required inside the bathhouses.

A picnic area and camping are available on the premises. It is sixteen miles to all other services.

Directions: From ID 55 in Donnelly, turn west and follow signs toward Rainbow Point Campground. Cross the Cascade Reservoir bridge. Follow Norwood Road and turn right onto Tamarack Road. After crossing the bridge at Tamarack Store turn right onto gravel road FS 186, bear left at the "Y", and follow FS 186 as it starts north, curves west, and then goes south. Watch for the hot spring on the west side of FS 186, 3.5 miles south of the intersection of FS 245 and FS 186.

GPS: N 44.68216 W 116.22919

Photo by Bob Seal

Photo by Bob Seal

We've been using this photo for Waterhole Lodge for many years because the owner says it's his favorite and he doesn't think he could take a better one.

489   WATERHOLE LODGE
PO Box 37   208 634-7758
Lake Fork, ID 83635

Dance floor, bar, lodge, and unique hot tubs with a spectacular view of the mountains. Located five miles south of McCall.

Two redwood hydrojet tubs In covered patios with one side that opens on a mountain view and three newer outdoor tubs have temperatures range from 102-106°. The water is treated with chlorine or bromine. Each unit has an inside, heated dressing room.

A cafe, tavern, rooms, overnight camping, RV hookups and a coin-op laundry are available on the premises. The whole place can be leased by private groups for celebrations, office parties, etc. A store and service station are within five blocks. Visa and MasterCard are accepted. Phone for rates, reservations, and directions.

490   KRIGBAUM HOT SPRINGS

●   **East of the town of Meadows**

Primitive hot springs and soaking pool on the east bank of Goose Creek, surrounded by Payette National Forest. Elevation 4,000 feet. Open all year.

Natural mineral water flows out of a spring at 102° and is piped to a volunteer-built, rock-and-cement pool where the temperatures range from 85-95°, depending on weather conditions. The apparent local custom is clothing optional.

There are no services available on the premises. It is two miles to a store, service station, overnight camping, and RV hookups and nine miles to a motel and restaurant.

Directions: On ID 55, go one mile east from Packer Johns Cabin State Park and turn north on FS 4553 near mile marker 152, a gravel road that runs along the east bank of Goose Creek. Just before the road crosses a bridge over Goose Creek, park and hike 300 yards north along the east bank to the pool.

Source map: *Payette National Forest.*
GPS: N 44.5753 W 116.1215

Photo by Bob Seal

491 ZIM'S HOT SPRINGS
PO Box 314   208 347-9447
■ **New Meadows, ID 83654**

Family owned plunge and picnic grounds in an agricultural valley surrounded by pines. The Little Salmon River runs through the property and the spectacular Granite Mountains provide the view. Elevation 4,200 feet. Open all year.

Natural mineral water flows out of an artesian well at 151° and is cooled as it is sprayed into the chlorine-treated pools. The temperature in the outdoor swimming pool ranges from 90-100° and from 103-106° in the outdoor soaking pool. Bathing suits are required.

Locker rooms, snacks, picnic area, overnight camping, and RV hookups are available on the premises. Fishing and winter sports are close by. A store, service station, and motel are located within four miles. Visa and MasterCard are accepted.

Directions: From the town of New Meadows, take US 95 four miles north, then follow signs to the plunge.

492 THE LODGE AT RIGGINS HOT SPRINGS
PO Box 1247   208 628-3785
■ **Riggins, ID 83549**

Secluded 155-acre luxury resort on the banks of the Salmon River, ten miles east of Riggins. Elevation 1,800 feet. Open all year.

Natural mineral water flows out of an artesian well at 140° and is piped to the recently remodeled soaking pool and enclosed spa. Water temperature in the flow-though spa is maintained at 105-108° without chlorination. Water temperature in the flow-through pool is maintained at 92-97° with a minimum of chlorination. The pools are open only to registered guests. Bathing suits are required.

Luxurious rooms with private baths are available in the main lodge and in a new three unit cabin. Meals and beverages included with the room rate. A stocked trout pond, a bathhouse with game room, and a conference center are available on the premises. Access to the Salmon River whitewater provides rafting, steelhead fishing, and jetboat excursions. Horses can be rented nearby. Visa and MasterCard are accepted.

Phone for rates, reservations, and directions.

Photos by Bob Seal

493   BURGDORF HOT SPRINGS
208 636-3036
◼   McCall, ID 83638

Picturesque, mountain-rustic resort without electricity or telephone, surrounded by Payette National Forest. Elevation 6,000 feet. Open all year. During the winter you can get there by snowmobile or cross-country skis.

Natural mineral water flows out of a spring at 112° and directly into and through a fifty by seventy-five-foot sandy-bottom swimming pool that averages 104° at the feed end and 98° at the outflow. The pool is about five-feet deep and requires no chemical treatment. There is also a small children's pool. The pools are open twenty-four hours a day to registered guests and 10AM-9PM for day use. Bathing suits are required during the daytime.

Twelve cabins with outdoor plumbing are available on the premises. Called "camping in a cabin" you need to bring your own bedding, food, cooking utensils, etc. Pack it in and out, and bring only biodegradable toiletries. There is also a small store with cold drinks, snacks, and some grocery items.

Overnight camping is within one-quarter of a mile. Check with the Payette National Forest Service in McCall for information. It is thirty miles to McCall and all other services. Hiking, skiing, snowmobiling, and boating are nearby. No credit cards are accepted.

You must write or phone first for reservations and information on current status and what to bring. For wintertime pick-up by snowmobile, write to the resort managers, Richard and Elizabeth Tidmarsh, General Delivery, McCall, ID 83638.

As far back as 1862 this was a favored resort by the folks who came to stay. There is still no electricity and the cabins use woodstoves for heat and kerosene lamps for light.

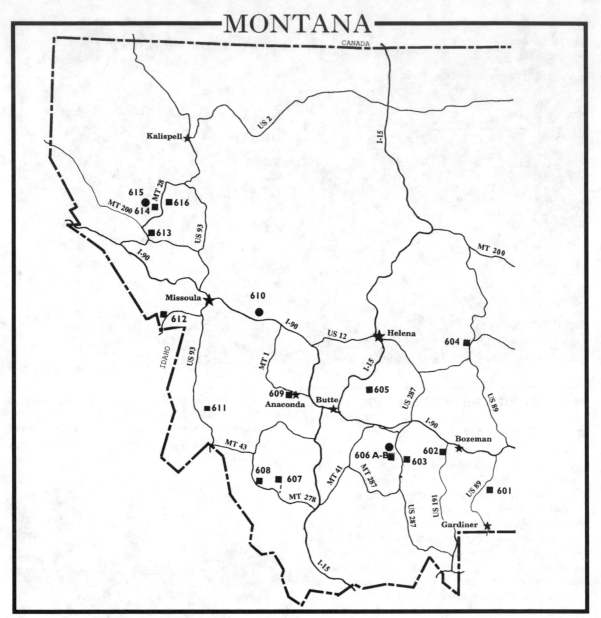

MONTANA

CANADA

This map was designed to be used with a standard highway map.

MAP SYMBOLS

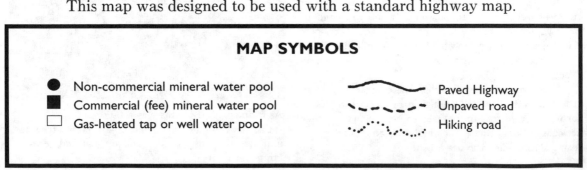

● Non-commercial mineral water pool

■ Commercial (fee) mineral water pool

☐ Gas-heated tap or well water pool

〰 Paved Highway

- - - Unpaved road

····· Hiking road

Courtesy of Chico Hot Springs Lodge

601   CHICO HOT SPRINGS LODGE
PO Drawer D   **406 333-4933**
■ **Pray, MT 59065**

Large, year-round resort established in 1900, surrounded by Gallatin National Forest. Elevation 5,200 feet. Open all year.

Natural mineral water flows out of several springs at 118° and is piped into a nearly Olympic-size, open-air pool maintained at 98°. The adjacent covered soaking pool averages 105°. One private-space hot tub, rented separately, is held at 105°. All pools operate on a flow-through basis and are available to the public as well as to resort guests. There is a wheelchair ramp through the poolside grill, and rooms are handicap accessible. Bathing suits are required.

Accommodations are available in the Main Lodge, the newer Lower Lodge, motel, log cabins, and condominiums. The resort offers dining in the Chico Inn and more casual fare in the Poolside Grille, a saloon with live entertainment on weekends, horseback riding, mountain bike and cross-country ski rentals, dogsled treks, and summer raft trips. It is three miles to a store with gas pumps and about eight miles to a full-service campground. Major credit cards are accepted.

Directions: Located approximately 23 miles south of Livingston and 31 miles north of Gardiner (the north entrance to Yellowstone Park). From the town of Emigrant on US 89, turn southeast on Murphy Lane (SR 362), go .8 miles to the stop sign, then left on East River Rd. (SR 540). Go .5 miles, then take the first right onto the Chico Road (SR 542). Resort is 1.6 miles up the road.

602   BOZEMAN HOT SPRINGS
81123 Gallatin Rd.   **406 587-3030**
■ **Bozeman, MT 59715**

Tree-shaded KOA campground with mineral water pools. Elevation 4,500 feet. Open all year. Pools closed from sundown Friday to sundown Saturday.

Natural mineral water flows out of a spring at 141° and is piped to an indoor pool building. The swimming pool is maintained at 90°, and adjoining soaking pools are maintained at temperatures ranging from 100-110°. There is also a 60° cold pool. All pools operate on a flow-through basis, including the cold tap water for controlling temperatures. Minimal chemical treatment is required. Pools are available to the public as well as to registered guests. Bathing suits are required.

Locker rooms, grocery store, laundromat, picnic area, RV hookups, and Kamper Kabins are available on the premises. It is one mile to a restaurant and service station and eight miles to a motel. Visa and MasterCard are accepted.

Location: On US 191, eight miles southwest of the town of Bozeman.   Photo by Justine Hill

Bozeman Hot Springs offers several different pools with varying temperatures for everyone to enjoy.

603 NORRIS HOT SPRINGS
PO Box 2916   **406 685-3303**
■ **Norris, MT 59745**

Small RV park in foothills below Tobacco Root Mountains. Elevation 5,000 feet. Open all year; days and times vary.

Natural mineral water flows out of artesian springs at 128°. The temperature in the outdoor soaking pool varies between 101° in the summer and 112° in the winter, depending on the weather. The water contains no sulfur, and only minimal chemical treatment is necessary because the pool operates on a flow-through basis. The pool is available to the public as well as to registered guests. Bathing suits are required.

A store, picnic area, overnight camping and RV hookups are available on the premises. It is one-quarter mile to a cafe, mini-mart and service station in Norris and seventeen miles south to a motel. No credit cards are accepted. Phone for open times.

Directions: From US 287 in the town of Norris, go .25 miles east on MT 84.

604 SPA MOTEL
PO Box 370   **406 547-3366**
■ **White Sulphur Springs, MT 59645**

Modern resort at the foot of the Castle Mountains. Elevation 5,100. Open all year.

Natural mineral water flows out of a spring at 120° and is piped to two pools that operate on a flow-through basis, requiring no chemical treatment. The pools are drained, cleaned, and refilled every night. The outdoor swimming pool is maintained at 94° in the summer and 102° in the winter. The indoor soaking pool is maintained at 105-106°. The deck around the pools, and the entire facility are geothermally heated. Handicap accessible. Bathing suits are required.

Rooms and a picnic area are available on the premises. It is less than five blocks to all other services. Visa and MasterCard are accepted.

Location: On US 89 at the west end of White Sulphur Springs.

Photo by Jayson Loam

Norris Hot Springs: This artesian spring operates during open hours offering a refreshing shower to go along with your soak.

Photo by Justine Hill

Boulder Hot Springs: Originally designated as a sanctuary by the Native Americans and consequently called Peace Valley, the hot springs lies at the edge of Deerlodge National Forest, home to bear, moose, deer, fox, antelope, and coyote. Renovations continue to be made to this 100-year-old grand hotel.

605 BOULDER HOT SPRINGS BED AND BREAKFAST

PO Box 930   406 225-4339

■ Boulder, MT 59632

Large historic resort built in 1888 is carefully being restored to its former charm. Nestled in the heart of Montana's Peace Valley, it was the first permanent building in the area. It is on 274 acres at the edge of Deerlodge National Forest and was designated by the Indians as a sanctuary where fighting was not permitted. Elevation 5,000 feet. Open all year. Pools are available on a day-use fee basis during the summer. Call about off-season hours.

Natural mineral water, pure enough to drink, flows out of several springs at temperatures between 150° and 175° and is piped to indoor and outdoor pools where it is cooled with water from the cold spring. Three newly tiled indoor pools with changing and shower area, offer men and women separate facilities for soaking. The women's bathhouse offers one hot pool maintained at 104° and a cooler one at 70°, while the men's bathhouse has one hot pool at 104°. All indoor plunges are large enough for at least thirty people. Water continually flows through, every four hours, and all pools are completely drained and filled nightly. There are saunas in both bathhouses, and bathing suits are optional. Pools are handicap accessible with some assistance.

The outdoor swimming pool is treated with bromine, and water temperatures range from 92-95°, depending on season. Bathing suits are required. All pools are handicap accessible with assistance.

Overnight accommodations, including meals, are offered to groups of fifteen or more for seminars, workshops, and retreats. There are guest rooms for up to sixty people. Breakfast is served daily. Seven rooms have been remodeled for bed and breakfast service. Several rooms are wheelchair accessible. Nearby attractions include plenty of hiking, skiing, fishing, panoramic views, Elkhorn Ghost Town, Lewis and Clark Caverns State Park, and the Radon Mines, known for their therapeutic qualities. Other services are available in nearby Boulder, Butte, or Helena. No pets or alcohol are allowed on the premises. Smoking outdoors only. Credit cards accepted.

Boulder Hot Springs is approximately midway between Helena and Butte on I-15. Airport pickup can be arranged. Phone for rates, reservations, and directions.

The swimming pool at *Potosi Hot Springs* is built right into the granite cliffs above Potosi Creek. The lodge was originally built in 1890.

606A   POTOSI HOT SPRINGS

PO Box 651	406 685-3594
■ Pony, MT 59747	800 770-0088

Newly constructed and well-equipped rustic log cabins and lodge on the site of an 1890s historic hotel originally built for gold miners of the area. Located in the Tobacco Root Mountains in Beaverhead National Forest. Elevation 7,000 feet. Open all year. Roads are kept plowed in winter.

Geothermal, sulfur-free mineral water flows up through the ground and emerges from granite cliffs directly into the large outdoor recreational pool where there is continual flow-through so that only minimal chlorination is necessary. The twenty- by sixty-foot pool is maintained at 84-85°. It is drained and scrubbed every two weeks, or more frequently if needed.

The Spring House, a private indoor soaking pool, enclosed by a Japanese-style insulated wooden hut, contains a rock pool that dates back to the 1890s. Water from a separate spring flows in by gravity at 90°, with a shut-off valve for draining and cleaning. Lanterns and candles are provided to complement the private dinners that can be ordered ahead. During the day sunlight streams in through a picturesque window.

Part of the runoff from the pools goes into the creek; and part is channeled through pipes into the lodge and cabins for heating. Spring water is used for drinking and showers. Pools are handicap accessible, with assistance.

A Japanese-style soaking tub with views of the nearby peaks and Potosi Creek is inside a Japanese-style hut. Dinner for two can be ordered in advance.

Management has an open policy about bathing suit requirements, leaving it up to the consensus of the bathers. Pools and facilities are available to registered guests only.

Facilities include a changing room near the pools, a lodge, and creek-front cabins that sleep up to six. One cabin is wheelchair accessible. Breakfast is served daily in the lodge and included in the overnight price. Dinner is by pre-arranged reservations only. Camping equipment is not included. Gas, grocery store, restaurant, and all other services are nine miles away in Harrison. Summer and winter outdoor activities are readily available on site and in the surrounding area. Reservations can be made through the resort. Visa, MasterCard, and personal checks are accepted.

Phone for rates, reservations, and directions.

Photos by Justine Hill

Photo by David Hummel

606B   NUPOTOSI HOT SPRINGS

● **South of the town of Pony**

Two small soaking pools in a beautiful valley in the Beaverhead National Forest with a clear view of the Tobacco Root Mountains. Elevation 6,600 feet. Open all year based on road conditions.

Natural mineral water flows directly up from the sides and bottom to fill the two rock-and-sand pools. The first pool, approximately nine- by six-feet is 101-106°. The second pool, seven feet in diameter is 98-103°. Bathing suits are optional although the pools are very popular in the summer and on weekends, and you may need to negotiate.

There are no services on the premises. It is about three-quarters of a mile to the Potosi Campground at the trailhead, and nine miles to all other services in Pony.

Directions: From the east end of Pony (consider this mile 0) take S. Willow Creek Rd 3.1 miles to a "T". Turn right (this is still called S. Willow Creek Rd.) and travel southwest. At mile point 6.7 the Potosi Lodge is on the right. Continue past the lodge to the campground at 8.6 miles. Take first campground entrance, pass the entry into the campground itself and proceed .2 miles to a turnout at C6, the trailhead. From the trailhead follow the well-worn trail to a fence.

Go through the gate, making sure to close it. Continue north along the edge of the private property. The trail roughly follows the fence line .75 miles through pines and meadows to the spring. The spring is surrounded by a pole fence, 10-12 meters below the trail.

Source map: *Beaverhead Deerlodge National Forest* (springs not listed).

GPS: N 45.58498 W 111.89670

Photo by Chris Andrews

Nupotosi is a rarity in Montana—a natural hot spring you can actually soak in. It is adjacent to private property and you must close a gate to get to it. Please do so, and also pack out what you pack in. Let's not lose this one.

607 ELKHORN HOT SPRINGS
PO Box 460514   **800 722-8978**
■ **Polaris, MT 59746**

Beautifully restored mountain resort, rustic lodge and cabins situated among the tall trees of Beaverhead National Forest. Elevation 7,300 feet. Open all year.

Natural mineral water flows out of six springs with temperatures ranging from 106-120°. The outdoor swimming pool is maintained at 88-95° and the outdoor soaking pool at 95-104°. There is one coed Roman sauna maintained at 105-108°. All pools are drained and refilled weekly. Pools are available to the public as well as to registered guests. Some areas are handicap accessible. Bathing suits are required.

Dressing rooms, restaurant, tent spaces, picnic area, overnight camping, and cabins are available on the premises. Horseback riding, backpacking, hunting, fishing, rock and mineral hunting, skiing, and snowmobile trails are available nearby. Cross-country ski rental is available on the premises. Pick-up service is provided from the city of Butte by prior arrangement. Visa and MasterCard are accepted.

Directions: Elkhorn Hot Springs is 43 miles northwest of Dillon, and 65 miles southwest of Butte. From I-15 three miles south of Dillon, take MT 278 west 27 miles to the large sign for Maverick Mt. Ski Area, Polaris, etc. Turn north and follow the Pioneer Scenic Byway 13 miles to the resort.

GPS: N 44.24507 W 114.88626   Photo by Justine Hill

Photo by Justine Hill

Jackson Hot Springs was discovered by Lewis and Clark in 1806 and mentioned in Clark's journal. Jackson is surrounded by several mountain ranges with numerous streams and high mountain lakes. Wildlife, including golden and bald eagles, is abundant.

608 JACKSON HOT SPRINGS
PO Box 808   **406 834-3151**
■ **Jackson, MT 59736**

Renovated lodge and cabins on the main street of a small town. Log construction, knotty pine interiors, and a massive stone fireplace in the main lodge add to the rustic warmth and western charm. Elevation 6,400 feet. Open all year.

Natural mineral water flows out of a spring at 137° and is piped to cabins and a large thirty- by seventy-five-foot outdoor pool. The temperature in the pool is maintained at 98-100° and operates on a flow- through basis. Water temperatures in cabin bathtubs can be controlled by adding cold tap water as needed. The swimming pool is available to the public as well as to registered guests. Bathing suits are required.

Facilities include dressing rooms, lodge complex with 16 cabins, a full-service restaurant, large western-style bar, and dance hall. Overnight camping and RV hookups are available on the premises. It is one block to a store and service station. Visa and MasterCard are accepted.

Location: On MT 278 on the main street in the town of Jackson.

609   FAIRMONT HOT SPRINGS RESORT
1500 Fairmont Rd   **406 797-3241**
■   **Anaconda, MT 59711**

A five-hundred acre, full service resort cradled by the Continental Divide. Elevation 5,300. Open all year.

Natural mineral water flows out of a spring at 160° and is piped to a 350-foot enclosed water slide and a group of pools, where it is treated with chlorine. The indoor and outdoor swimming pools are maintained at 80-85° and the indoor and outdoor soaking pools at 105°. There are also men's and women's steam rooms. Facilities are available to the public as well as to registered guests. Pool area is wheel chair accessible, as are specially equipped guest rooms. Bathing suits are required.

Locker rooms, two restaurants, lounge, rooms, mini-zoo, tennis, golf course, are available on the premises. Overnight camping, RV hookups, country store, and gas station are nearby. Fishing, snowmobiling, hunting, horse-back riding, and skiing are all close by. Visa, MasterCard, Discover, and American Express are accepted.

Directions: From I-90 12 miles west of Butte, take the Gregson-Fairmont exit (#211) and follow signs to the resort.

Fairmont Hot Springs: A 350-foot enclosed water slide, along with a mini-zoo, makes the Fairmont a popular destination resort for families with children. Adults can entertain themselves with golf, tennis, and a video casino right on the premises.

Courtesy of Fairmont Hot Springs Resort

610 NIMROD SPRINGS

● **East of the town of Clinton**

A popular warm swimming hole along the north side of I 90 with an underground room accessible only by the adventurous. Located at the base of the Garnet Mountains. Elevation 3,600 feet. Open all year.

Natural mineral water around 70° flows over the edge of a cliff into a large pool, eight-feet deep in places. In the summer, a small room inside the cliff is accessible by swimming under the water to get into the room. A suit seems preferred based on the proximity to the road, but it is not uncommon to encounter skinny dippers.

There are no services on the premises. It is approximately seven miles to Beaver Tail Hill Campground, and all other services can be found either in Bearmouth, seven miles away, or in Clinton, fifteen miles away.

Directions: The spring is on the north side of I 90 at milemarker 136.7. It is located in the middle of a large "S" bend in the interstate. Parking is a problem and the authorities suggest you not park within the "S". Instead, park along the interstate, making sure you are completely off the shoulder and not blocking traffic. You may need to park as far as .5 miles away. There are signs near the springs prohibiting parking.

Sources Maps: *Lolo National Forest;* USGS *Bearmouth* (springs not listed on either map).

GPS: N 46.70534 W 113.45633

Photos by Chris Andrews

Summertime! The weather is hot, but this large swimming hole offers a refreshing waterfall and soak. For those of you brave souls there is also a room inside this cave which can only be reached by swimming under water.

Photos courtesy of Lost Trails Hot Springs

Known in previous times as Gallogly Springs, this resort has a colorful history. For years it was a secluded stopping place for travelers crossing the Continental Divide at the pass. The old Indian trail climbs about 2,000 feet in three miles, making it a very difficult trek. People would often stop to rest at the springs before starting the long climb. Later, farmers taking their produce to market would stop at the springs for the night. Nowadays, home-style cooking and a natural mineral water pool make it a great destination resort.

---

611 LOST TRAILS HOT SPRINGS RESORT

| 8321 Hwy 93 S | 406 821-3574 |
| Sula, MT 59871 | 800 825-3574 |

Historic rustic mountain resort, located on beautifully forested private land within the Bitterroot National Forest. Elevation 5,000 feet. Open all year. Call ahead in winter when pools may be closed Monday and Tuesday.

Natural mineral water bubbles up at 108-110° and flows by gravity through pipes at 100 gallons per minute to a large twenty-one- by seventy-foot outdoor swimming pool. Runoff is diverted to the creek below. Inflow pipes are laid under the concrete surrounding the pools so they don't ice up in winter. There is an adjoining ten-inch deep, ten- by twenty-one-foot kiddy pool. The pools are covered by a dome in winter, keeping the air temperature warm enough to grow bananas or oranges.

Indoors is a sauna and a fiberglass hot tub in a separate wood-paneled room. The water temperature is maintained at 106°. Pools and sauna are available on a day-use basis.

Facilities include dressing rooms, rustic housekeeping cabins, a motel, two lodges which can accommodate large groups and family reunions of up to thirty people, full bar with casino, restaurant, fireplace, children's play area, and a convenience store. There are also RV spaces with hookups. A National Forest campground is two-tenths of a mile north of the resort.

Activities in the surrounding wilderness area include hiking, alpine and Nordic skiing, fishing, backpacking, horseback riding, and rafting. Snowmobiles and cross-country skis are available for rent at the resort. It is six miles to a post office/general store in Sula and twenty-five miles to all other services in Darby. Most major credit cards are accepted.

Location: On Hwy 93, 6 miles south of Sula, Montana, 6 miles north of the Montana-Idaho border at Lost Trails Pass. The resort is 88 miles south of Missoula, Montana and 55 miles north of Salmon, Idaho.

Photo by Bob Seal

Photo by Jayson Loam

Quinn's Paradise Resort: Fun is the key word for this family resort where kids and their parents can soak in the separate outdoor swimming and hydrojet pools.

612   LOLO HOT SPRINGS RESORT
■   38500 Highway 12   406 273-2290
    Lolo, MT 59847

An historic resort that has been restored and expanded, nestled in the heart of the Lolo National Forest near the Selway-Bitterroot Wilderness, 30 miles west of Missoula. Elevation 4,700 feet. Open all year.

Natural mineral water flows out of two springs at temperatures of 110° and 117° and is piped to two pools that are built directly over the springs themselves. Water is pumped up into the pools, and with continual flow-through, the water in each pool is completely changed every twenty-four hours, requiring only minimal chlorination. The large outdoor pool maintains a temperature of 92-98°. The covered soaking pool maintains a temperature of 103-105°. Bathing suits are required.

Facilities include dressing rooms, bathhouse, RV park, campground, tepees for rent, and a picnic area. Full-service restaurant; saloon with casino, mini-gift shop, and newly built rustic log motel (406 273-2201) are available on the premises. Most facilities are open year-round. Recreational activities include hiking, mountain biking, horseback riding, snowmobiling, and cross-country skiing. Snowmobile rental are available from the lodge. Call during heavy snow regarding status of RV park and campgrounds. Credit cards accepted. All other services are available twenty-five miles east in Lolo. Phone for rates and reservations.

Location: On US 12, 25 miles west of Lolo, MT, seven miles east of the Montana-Idaho border.

613   QUINN'S PARADISE RESORT:
         A NATURAL HOT SPRINGS
■   PO Box 219   406 826-3150
    Paradise, MT 59856

Complete family resort on the banks of the Clark Fork River. Elevation 2,700 feet. Open all year.

Natural mineral water flows out of a spring at 120°. The outdoor swimming pool is treated with chlorine and maintained at a temperature of 88°. The outdoor hydrojet pool is maintained at 100° and operates on a flow-through basis so that only minimal chemical treatment of the water is needed. There are two indoor, private-space fiberglass tubs in which the water temperature can be controlled by the customer. These pools are drained and refilled after each use, so that no chemical treatment is necessary. Pools are available to the public as well as to registered guests. Bathing suits are required except in private spaces.

Dressing rooms, cafe, bar, store, rooms and cabins, overnight camping, RV hookups, and fishing are available on the premises. It is eleven miles to the service station in Plains (on MT 200). Most major credit cards are accepted.

Location: On MT 135, three miles south of the junction with MT 200, which is east of St. Regis.

Courtesy of Symes Hot Springs

614 SYMES HOT SPRINGS HOTEL AND MINERAL BATHS

PO Box 651   406 741-2361
209 Wall St.
■   Hot Springs, MT 59845   888 305-3106

Historic, recently restored hotel with a long tradition of hot mineral water baths and comfortable lodgings. Elevation 2,900 feet. Open all year.

Natural mineral water flows out of an artesian well at 80-90° and is heated as needed for use in soaking tubs to temperatures of 105-107°. There are seven individual soaking tubs in the men's bathhouse and six in the women's bathhouse. Temperature is controllable within each tub, and no chemical treatment is added. The hot water, at temperatures between 102-104°, also fills the twelve-foot octagon pool that spills into a lower twenty-foot square lower pool. Minimal chlorination is required. Soaks are available to the public for a fee, as well as to registered guests. Mineral water is piped to many of the hotel rooms. Bathing suits are required in public areas.

Shower rooms, twenty-eight hotel rooms (ten with mineral water), and a new, deluxe hot tub suite with a six-person tub, a full sauna, and kitchenette that will sleep four. An antique shop, espresso bar, an art studio, kitchen facilities, small conference room, hair salon and bike rentals can also be found at the hotel. Massage therapy is also available. It is two blocks to restaurants and a cafe, store, and service station. Credit cards are accepted.

Directions: From MT 382 northeast of St. Regis, follow signs to the town of Hot Springs and then to the hotel.

You can still enjoy a soak in a claw-footed bathtub from 1928 when the hotel was built, or enjoy these new mineral water outdoor pools. In the summer you may be able to enjoy an open-air concert at the resort.

Photos by Chris Andrews

615   CAMAS SPRINGS

● **North side of the town of Hot Springs**

Two nice concrete soaking pools and a mud pool in a park-like setting on the north side of Hot Springs, Montana on the Flathead Indian Reservation. Elevation 3500 feet. Open all year.

Natural mineral water from an artesian well at 115° is piped to a nine by eighteen-foot concrete pool with a sandy bottom and a bench to sit on where you can enjoy the 102-104° water. It also fills a round, sandy-bottom eight-foot concrete pool whose temperatures range from 102-106°. The temperature is controlled by a caretaker who comes around to check the pools every day. The mud bath area has benches to lie on and a hot water hose to clean off you and the area around. The pools would be handicap accessible with assistance. Bathing suits are required.

All services are within a quarter of a mile in the town of Hot Springs. The closest campground, Rainbow Lake, is twelve miles away.

Source maps: USGS *Hot Springs; Lolo National Forest* (springs not shown).

GPS: N 47.61432 W 114.66891

Originally these were the source pools for the old Camas tribal bathhouse which closed around 1990. Said to be the second most healing water in the world, next to Baden Baden in Germany. Worth wearing a suit for.

Photos by Chris Andrews

A tribal treaty stipulates that no admission would ever be charged to soak in the water. However, donations help to keep this area pristine.

After letting the mud dry on your skin, rinse off with the warm water from the hose provided for this purpose. You then might want to soak in the wonderful water again.

Photos by Chris Andrews

616 WILD HORSE HOT SPRINGS
PO Box 629   406 741-3777
■ Hot Springs, MT 59845

Well-maintained, family rent-a-tub establishment with overnight facilities surrounded by rolling foothills. Elevation 2,750 feet. Open all year.

Natural mineral water flows out of an artesian well at 124° and is piped to the bathhouse building. There are six large indoor soaking pools in private rooms, each with steam bath, sauna, shower, and toilet. Pool water temperature is controllable by each customer up to 110°. The pools are scrubbed down frequently, so no chemical treatment is needed. Bathing suits are not required in private rooms. Geothermal heat is used in all buildings.

Picnic area, overnight camping, and RV hookups are available on the premises. Overnight accommodations include a soak. It is six miles to all other services. No credit cards are accepted.

Directions: From MT 28, 2.5 miles north of Hot Springs junction, follow signs 2 miles east on the gravel road to the resort.

Photo by Jayson Loam

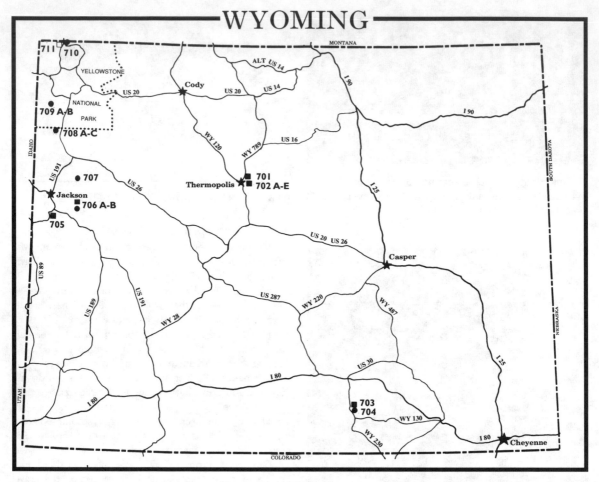

WYOMING

This map was designed to be used with a standard highway map.

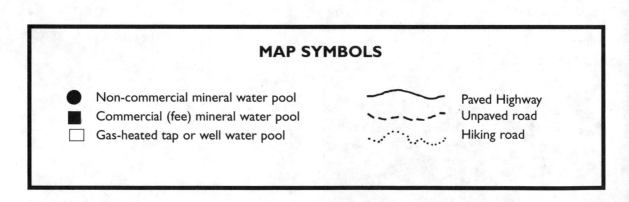

MAP SYMBOLS

- ● Non-commercial mineral water pool
- ■ Commercial (fee) mineral water pool
- □ Gas-heated tap or well water pool

- ∿ Paved Highway
- – – – Unpaved road
- ····· Hiking road

701   FOUNTAIN OF YOUTH RV PARK
■   PO Box 711   307 864-3265
Thermopolis, WY 82443

Well-kept RV park featuring a unique, large soaking pool. Elevation 4,300 feet. Open March 1 to October 31.

Natural mineral water flows out of the historic Sacajawea Well at the rate of over one million gallons per day. Some of this 130° water is channeled through a cooling pond into a 200-foot-long soaking pool where the temperature varies from 104° at the inflow end to 99° at the outflow. A special ramp makes the pool handicap accessible. The pool is available only to registered day and overnight campers. Bathing suits are required.

Rest rooms, showers, picnic sites, laundry, RV supplies, overnight camping, and RV hookups are available on the premises. It is two miles to all other services. Visa and MasterCard are accepted.

Location: On US 20, two miles north of the town of Thermopolis.

Courtesy of Fountain of Youth

These families are enjoying the largest mineral pool in Wyoming and the third largest in the world.

It is probable that the well that fills this 235-foot by 72-foot pool taps the same hot mineral water reservoir as that which supplies the Big Spring in Thermopolis. The water flow is so enormous that the pool water is exchanged every 11 hours. The well was originally drilled in 1918 in a search for oil. Instead, hot mineral water came gushing out under such pressure that the derrick was destroyed.

Thermopolis, a Greek word for "Hot City," is located next to Hot Springs State Park, which offers several different places to enjoy a hot mineral soak. All of the establishments on the grounds are supplied with natural mineral water from the Big Springs. Big Horn Hot Springs releases 2.8 million gallons daily and is one of the largest mineral springs in the world.

Walkways have been provided through the large tufa terraces that have been built up by mineral deposits from the spring over the centuries. These terraces, hot waterfalls, a dinosaur museum and the state's bison herd—in addition to a nice relaxing soak—makes the trip to the park, only two hours from Yellowstone, well worthwhile.

This square mile of land was presented to the State of Wyoming by the Federal Government after it had been purchased from the Shoshone and Arapahoe Indians in 1896. Annually, in August, the Shoshone Indians set up their tepees and reenact the "Wedding of the Waters," portraying the sale of the springs.

For more information, contact the Thermopolis Chamber of Commerce, 800-SUN-N-SPA.

Courtesy of the Chamber of Commerce

702B   TEPEE SPA
PO Box 750   307 864-9250
■ **Thermopolis, WY 82443**

The outdoor and indoor swimming pools are maintained at 92-96° year-round, and the indoor soaking pool is maintained at 104°. The indoor steambath is maintained at 110-115°. There are three outdoor hot tubs with temperatures varying from 100-104° and indoor/outdoor water slides. Also, there are giant indoor and outdoor water slides, and a kiddie pool. All pools operate on a flow-through basis, so only minimal chemical treatment is needed. Ramps and railings make the hot tubs handicap accessible. Bathing suits are required.

A steam room, dry sauna, picnic area, locker rooms and a snack bar and gift shop are available on the premises. It is also possible to book a massage. Visa and MasterCard are accepted.

702A   STATE BATH HOUSE
State Park   307 864-3765
■ **Thermopolis, WY 82443**

The outdoor and indoor soaking pools are maintained at 104°. The temperature in sixteen (eight men's and eight women's) individual soaking tubs is adjustable by the person using the tub. All pools use minimally chlorinated, flow-through mineral water. No charge is made for pool or tub use.

Changing rooms are available, and bathing suits are required in the communal pools. There is a nominal charge for renting suits or towels. No credit cards are accepted.

A treaty between the Shoshone and Arapaho nations and the United States specified that some of the waters were to be free to all. The State Bath House (picture, left) honors this commitment.

702C STAR PLUNGE
PO Box 627   307 864-3771
Thermopolis, WY 82443

The outdoor swimming pool is maintained at 92-96° and the indoor swimming pool is maintained at 96-98°. The hot pool also has a hydrojet section that is maintained at 104°. Included are an indoor and an outdoor waterslide open throughout the year. The coed steambath is maintained at 118°. All pools are flow-through, requiring only minimal chemical treatment. Bathing suits are required.

Locker rooms and a snack bar are available on the premises. No credit cards are accepted.

702D PLAZA HOTEL/QUALITY INN
PO Box 671   888 919-9009
Thermopolis, WY 82443

Due to open in Spring, 1999; currently accepting reservations.

Plans include both hot mineral water and fresh water pools, complete remodeling of thirty-six rooms, eighteen of which are suites.

702E HOLIDAY INN
PO Box 1323   307 864-3131
Thermopolis, WY 82443

Conventional, major hotel with a unique adaptation of men's and women's bathhouses. Each bathhouse has private spaces for four individual soaking tubs, two saunas and two steambaths. The private spaces are rented to couples, even though they are in the men's and women's bathhouses.

The indoor soaking tubs can be temperature controlled up to 110°, use natural mineral water, and are drained after each use so that no chemical treatment is needed. The outdoor hydrojet pool also uses natural mineral water and is maintained at a temperature of 104°. The outdoor swimming pool uses gas-heated, chlorine-treated tap water and is maintained at a temperature of 81-84°. There is also a private indoor hydropool. All pools and the athletic club facilities are available to the public as well as to registered guests. Bathing suits are required in all outdoor public areas.

Restaurant and hotel rooms are available on the premises. All season sports and equipment rentals are available at the inn or close by. Visa, MasterCard, American Express, and Carte Blanche are accepted.

Courtesy of Holiday Inn

Present-day explorers have the advantage of a warm, relaxing soak after a hard day fishing or hunting, as did the early settlers to this area.

Courtesy of Saratoga Inn Resort

Beautifully landscaped grounds on the outside offer tastefully appointed lodge rooms on the inside, replete with featherbeds, handmade lamps, locally crafted furniture and prints of the old west.

703 THE SARATOGA INN RESORT AND HOT SPRINGS SPA

■ 601 E Pic Pike Rd.   307 326-5261
Saratoga, WY 82331

Located along the pristine North Platte River, the Inn boasts one of the Rocky Mountains' most beautiful sites with challenging golf courses, guided river and mountain lake and stream fishing, guided scenic riverboat tours, unforgettable Sierra horseback riding, tennis, snowmobiling, cross country skiing and hot mineral water pools.

Hot mineral baths are located right outside your lodge room with three special, tepee covered baths for private soaking, with temperatures ranging from 105-112°. A twenty-five yard mineral spring swimming pools is located off the main soaking tub and is kept at 100°, with chlorine added as needed. Pool use is reserved for registered guests. Bathing suits are required.

The Inn offers an enticing menu selected by their master chef who has been featured in several gourmet magazines, a micro-brewery offering hand-crafted beers brewed on-site, a major western outfitter, and the Hot Springs Spa, offering full, luxurious body treatments and massage. Corporate retreats are a specialty in these unique surroundings. Credit cards accepted.

Location: Off of Highway 139 on one of the "ten best road tour drives in the US," Saratoga is only three and one-half hours from Denver, one hour from Laramie and two hours from Cheyenne. A corporate-jet airport is located one mile south of the resort.

Hobo Pool: Thanks to the town council, there's not only a fenced swimming pool which charges a fee, but a large soaking pool that is free to everyone.

704 HOBO POOL

● **In the town of Saratoga**

An improved but unfenced soaking pool, newly enhanced with a wall of moss rock, and a fenced municipal swimming pool located on the banks of the North Platte River. Elevation 6,800 feet. Open all year.

Natural mineral water flows out of the source spring at 115°. A large cement soaking pool (free to the public) maintains a temperature of 100-110°. Volunteers have channeled the soaking pool runoff into shallow rock pools along the edge of the river. A daily charge is made for the use of the swimming pool, which is maintained at 90° and is closed in the winter. Bathing suits are required.

There are showers, changing rooms, and public rest rooms on the premises. It is three blocks to all services. No credit cards are accepted.

Directions: On WY 130 in the town of Saratoga, watch for the HOBO POOL sign, then follow the signs four blocks east to the pool.

Located on the Snake River (visible below behind the pool) Astoria is a popular stopping place for visitors to Jackson Hole, Grand Tetons, and Yellowstone.

705 ASTORIA MINERAL HOT SPRINGS
(see map below)

Star Route, Box 18   307 733-2659
Jackson, WY 83001

Large, well-kept RV resort on the south bank of the Snake River. Elevation 5,000 feet. Open mid-May to Labor Day.

Natural mineral water flows out of a spring at 104° and is piped to an outdoor swimming pool where it cools naturally and is maintained at a temperature of 95°. The pool is drained and cleaned twice a week, at which time the bottom and sides are treated with chlorine. There is a also a separate kiddie pool. The pools are available to the public as well as to registered guests who get a discount for pool use. No flotation devices are allowed in the pool. A new shower and restroom are handicap accessible. Bathing suits are required.

Locker rooms, picnic area, volleyball, basketball, tent spaces, RV hookups, grocery store, and river raft trips are available on the premises. Bathing suits and towels are available for rent. It is three miles to a service station, store, and motel in Hoback Junction and four miles to a cafe. Visa and MasterCard are accepted.

Location: On US 26/89, 17 miles south of the town of Jackson.

Photos by Justine Hill

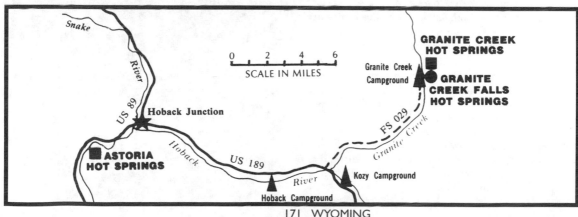

Photo by Phil Wilcox

706A   GRANITE CREEK HOT SPRINGS
(see map on page 171)

■   East of Hoback Junction

Part of a major bonanza for lovers of natural beauty and natural mineral water. Elevation 7,000 feet. Open all year, including the winter season for those who have snow cats.

Natural mineral water flows out of a spring at 112° and tumbles directly into a large cement pool built by the CCC in the 1930s. Cold stream water is added as needed to maintain the pool temperature of 95° in the summer and 105° in the winter. The pool is drained and refilled each day, so no chemical treatment is needed. Bathing suits are required.

Changing rooms and rest rooms are available on the premises, which is operated under a lease with the Forest Service. Suits and towels are for rent. The site is closed and gates are locked from 8 PM to one hour before dark. A day-use fee is charged. There is a picnic area with firepits near the pool and Granite Creek Campground, a large, wooded, creekside campground is .5 miles away. Primitive camping is available on open stretches at creekside along the ten-mile gravel road between the highway and the springs. It is eighteen miles to a cafe and motel and twenty-two miles to all other services.

Granite Creek Hot Springs was built by the Civilian Conservation Corps (CCC) in 1933 and is currently operated under a special-use permit granted by the Bridger-Teton National Forest.

Directions: From Jackson, drive 13 miles south on US 191/189 to Hoback Junction. Bear left and continue 11.4 miles on US 191/189 to Granite Creek Road. Turn left (consider this point 0). Bear right at 1.4 miles and continue 9.2 miles into the parking area.

Photo by Justine Hill

Photos by Chris Andrews

706B GRANITE CREEK FALLS HOT SPRINGS (see map on page 171)
● East of Hoback Junction

A series of primitive rock-and-sand soaking pools are located along the creek at the foot of Granite Creek Falls. A small waterfall at 118° seeps up from underground and flows down a creek bank adjacent to Granite Falls and into a series of volunteer-built pools where temperatures range from 96-110°. Temperature can be controlled by diverting the water or by mixing it with cold creek water. These pools must be rebuilt after each annual high-water washout. Although the spring is partly visible from the road, the apparent local custom is clothing optional, although in popular summer months bathing suits seem to be preferred.

Several trails lead to these primitive pools. From the fee-area concrete pool, a trail leads off to the left just before the bridge over the creek. It is a ten to fifteen minute walk along this narrow trail to a spot above the falls where a steep trail heads off to the right down to the creek where volunteers rebuild a variety of pools each year. These pools can also be reached from the parking area for Granite Falls, which is approximately ten miles in from the main highway and one-quarter mile before the fee-area pool. To reach the pools, it is necessary to ford the very swiftly flowing creek. Do not attempt to ford the creek during high water. A third trail leads up from the Girl Scout Camp parking and trailhead area, which is eight miles in from the highway along the gravel road, before the falls.

Directions: From Jackson, drive 13 miles south on US 191/189 to Hoback Junction. Bear left and continue 11.4 miles on US 191/189 to Granite Creek Road. Turn left (consider this point 0). Bear right at 1.4 miles. At 8.7 miles turn left and drive towards the falls. Park anywhere at the edge of the road and walk the remaining 200 yards to the base of the falls.

Source map: USGS *Granite Falls*.
GPS: N 43.36507 W 110.44347

Photo by Chris Andrews

Whether there are patches of snow on the hills surrounding the pool and the Grand Tetons, or the pool is surrounded by summer wildflowers, people enjoy soaking here all year except in severe winter months.

707   KELLY WARM SPRINGS

● **Northeast of Jackson**

Large warm pond with a gorgeous view of the Grand Tetons, located within the national park. Wonderful for a summer soak. Elevation 6,700 feet. Open all year except for the worst part of winter.

Natural mineral water flows directly into a large gravel-bottom pool up to eight feet deep in an open meadow. The water temperature of 81° makes this an ideal hot-weather soak, albeit a bit cool in winter. The pool is adjacent to the road, so bathing suits are advisable.

There are no services available on the premises. The nearest campground, Gros Ventre, is five miles away in Grand Teton National Park. All other services are twenty miles away in Jackson.

Directions: From Jackson, drive north on US 189/191 about 7 miles to Gros Ventre Road. Turn right on Gros Ventre Road (consider this point 0). Drive through the town of Kelly following the left curve which comes up at about 7 miles. At 8.2 miles you will come to Gros Ventre Rd. Turn right (east). The springs are .4 of a mile and are clearly visible from the road.

Source maps: USGS *Shadow Mountain*. *Bridger Teton National Forest.*

GPS: N 43.64006 W 110.61579

Photo by Bob Seal

HUCKLEBERRY HOT SPRINGS

The springs were originally developed as a commercial swimming area in the 1960s and continued to operate, free of charge, until the pool was closed by the Park Service in 1983 to let the area return to its natural state. This action included bulldozing the swimming pool and removing the access bridge over Polecat Creek. Now it is necessary to wade Polecat Creek in order to get to the springs from the parking area at the end of the old access road. Trails in the area are not maintained.

Thanks to one of our readers, we can now suggest an alternate path to the pools when spring runoff is high and getting to the pools is not safe when you have to wade across the river.

Photo by Chris Andrews

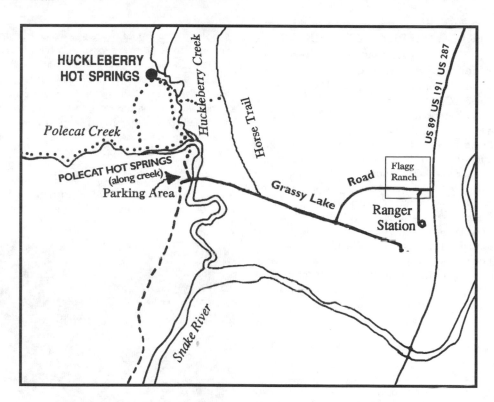

Since the last edition of the book, Flagg Ranch has been moved north of the Ranger Station. You now need to go through Flagg Ranch to access Grassy Lake Road. An alternate path to the springs in case Polecat Creek is too high to cross near the parking area is to go back and take the obvious horse trail along the ridge above the creek. Walk for about fifteen minutes and turn left on a well-worn foot path. Continue another ten minutes to reach the pools.

Photos by Chris Andrews

708A HUCKLEBERRY HOT SPRINGS
(see map on previous page)
● **North of the town of Jackson**

Large group of primitive hot springs along the north bank of Polecat Creek within Grand Teton National Park, near the south entrance to Yellowstone National Park. Elevation 6,800 feet. Open all year.

Natural mineral water flows out of many springs at temperatures up to 130°, cooling as it follows various channels to the creek. The hottest and most spectacular flow is where hot water bubbles up into a large pond, flows over hot lava rocks, and tumbles down in a hot waterfall into a soaking pool at 110°. Runoff goes into Huckleberry Creek. The entire creek below this point has hot water, and volunteers have built small rock-and-mud soaking pools at several places where the water is in the 100-105° range. Although this is close to Yellowstone, there are very few visitors, so the apparent local custom is clothing optional. However, it is advisable to have a bathing suit handy in case anyone objects to skinny-dippers.

There are no services available on the premises. There is a commercial campground within one mile, and all other services are available at Flagg Ranch, 1.25 miles away. Flagg Ranch, a private operation, does allow the Park Service to have a Visitors Information office on the premises where some information is provided on the springs and camping areas. Primitive camping areas are also available along Grassy Lake Road, past the turnoff for the springs.

Source map: USGS *Flagg Ranch*; Bridger-Teton National Forest Map (shows springs, but not trails). (Hot springs not shown on Grand Teton National Park map.)

Directions: Access Grassy Lake Road through Flagg Ranch Village. Immediately after crossing a bridge look for a parking pullout on the right. The trail begins here as an abandoned road. It is a short five-minute walk to Polecat Creek. Wade the creek and continue straight ahead for another 5 to 10 minutes.(See map for alternate route if creek is too high to wade across.) At a flat grassy area, one trail veers off to the right, leading to the hot creek. Another leads straight ahead to a flat area where water seeps out of the ground just above the scalding waterfall.

GPS: N 44.115 W 110.684

Photo by J. Russel Criswell

708B-C POLECAT HOT SPRINGS
(see Huckleberry map)
● **North of the town of Jackson**

Two groups of primitive log-and-rock soaking pools along Polecat Creek, near Huckleberry Creek and hot springs, with spectacular mountain views.

Directions: Driving and access are the same as for Huckleberry Hot Springs. From the parking area, follow the trail to Polecat Creek. After wading the creek, make an immediate left onto a trail which parallels Polecat Creek. It is a short five minute walk to the first group of pools at Lower Polecat.

B: Lower Polecat. A lovely, elaborately elevated log-and-rock soaking pool which is deep enough to sit in and large enough for eight-to-ten people stretched out. Water tumbles through the logs into the pool along the creek where, after mixing with the cool creek water, the soaking temperature is approximately 100°.

GPS: N 44.11199 W 110.70249

Upper Polecat: The marshy grasslands make this a difficult walk during wet weather. However, chances are good you will have the place to yourself.

C: Upper Polecat. Continue up the trail along the creek for another 15-20 minutes until the trail disappears in a large stand of pine tress. From here, Polecat Creek makes a sweeping curve to the left. Up ahead you will notice a few single pine trees at the creek's edge. Keep your eye on these. The hot pools are at the creek in this area. Walk through the stand of pines, over marshy grassland where the trail virtually disappears, and work your way toward the pine trees along the creek to the pools. (The area is very marshy and difficult to get to in the wet weather.) Hot water seeps out in two separate streams and flows into volunteer-built rock-and-log pools of varying sizes and temperatures as the hot water mixes with cool creek water. (One soaker suggested a stiff brush to clean some of the algae off the rocks.)

GPS: N 44.11199 W 110.68754

Photo by Steve Heerema

SHOSHONE GEYSER BASIN
In Yellowstone National Park

Several primitive, creekside soaking pools along a beautiful nine-mile trail from Kepler Cascades to the west end of Shoshone Lake.

Boiling hot natural mineral water erupts from geyser cones and bubbles out of hot springs, flowing to join nearby cold streams, the only legal places to put your body in Yellowstone's hot water. Rocks and sand have been arranged by volunteers to make small shallow pools where the two waters combine at temperatures tolerable to human skin. Be sure to check with the rangers to make sure which springs are legal to use.

Photos by Chris Andrews

709A   DUNANDA FALLS HOT SPRINGS

●   In Yellowstone National Park

Several small pools located below the 110-foot Dunanda Falls in a beautifully forested gorge within the Shoshone Geyser Basin area. Elevation 6,500 feet. Access depends on snowpack and spring runoff; could be late June to November.

Natural mineral water flows out of springs adjacent to the river below the falls. The 150° water flows through channels into several rock-and-sand pools at the river's edge, where the temperature can be controlled by mixing with the cold river water. The size and shape of the pools change frequently depending on the degree of flow. The apparent local custom is clothing optional.

There are no services at this location. However, there are several campgrounds in the Shoshone Lake and Shoshone Creek area for which camping permits are required. The springs are adjacent to a primitive campground. Cave Falls Campground is eight miles away. All other services are located twenty-five miles from the trailhead in Ashton, Idaho.

If you do not already have hiking guides and/or detailed maps of the area, obtain them when you apply for a camping permit. At that time, also ask about weather conditions and any other pertinent information.

Directions: From Ashton, Idaho (ID 20), drive east on Highway 47 and follow the signs 25 miles to the Bechler Ranger Station. This is the trail head for the relatively flat, 8.5 mile hike to Dunanda Falls.

GPS: N 44.24721 W 111.02392

Pack your camping gear, obtain a permit and be prepared to view magnificent *Dunanda Falls* and to soak in one of the adjacent hot pools.

709B   FERRIS FORK POOL

● **In Yellowstone National Park**

Considered by many to be the "ultimate in hot springs," these multiple rock pools are located half-way between Old Faithful and the Bechler River, one-half mile south of the main trail on a marked spur trail.

Natural mineral water at temperatures up to 190° discharges into the cold water of Shoshone Creek. A pleasant soak for two to three people is possible behind the rocks and logs. Two other similar locations exist nearby. One is a pool on a small side stream just below (south) of the main pool; the other is on Shoshone Creek, just upstream from the main pool. The apparent local custom is clothing optional.

Maps and directions are available from the Ranger Station, and a wilderness permit is required for this easy sixteen-mile one-way hike. There are nearby wilderness campgrounds for which a permit is also required.

GPS: N 44.28730 W 110.87882

Photos by Chris Andrews

Ferris Fork: The Bechler River flow reaches approximately one hundred degrees below this major spring.

MADISON CAMPGROUND WARM SPRING

- **In Yellowstone National Park**

There is no longer any access to the warm water flow in the campground.

---

710   BOILING RIVER

- **In Yellowstone National Park**

Turbulent confluence of hot mineral water and cold river water along the west bank of the Gardiner River, just below Park Headquarters at Mammoth Hot Spring. Elevation 5,500 feet. Open all year during daylight hours only.

Natural mineral water flows out of a very large spring at 140° and travels thirty yards through an open channel where it tumbles down the south bank of the Gardiner River. Volunteers have rearranged rocks in the river to control the flow of cold water in an eddy pocket where the hot and cold water churn into a swirling mixture that varies from 50-110°. Bathing suits are required.

Facilities include an enclosed pit toilet at the parking area, bear-proof trash receptacles, and a bicycle rack. All other services are available in Gardner, two and one-half miles north; or refer to the NPS Yellowstone Park map for the location of all services within the park.

Directions: On the North Entrance Road, 4 miles from Mammoth Hot Spring and 2.5 miles from the town of Gardiner, look for a large parking area on both sides of the road at the Montana-Wyoming state line and the 45th Parallel sign. Turn into the parking lot behind that sign on the east side of the road, and hike .5 miles upstream to where Boiling River cascades over the riverbank.

Photos by Chris Andrews

711   MAMMOTH HOT SPRINGS HOTEL
         AND CABINS
         MAMMOTH HOT SPRINGS   307 344-7311
❑   YELLOWSTONE NATIONAL PARK,
         WY   82190

Four fiberglass, hydrojet pools filled with chlorinated, electrically heated tap water behind high board fences adjoining four small cabins. Elevation 6,200 feet. Call for open times.

These pools are rented for public use by the hour during the winter. During the summer they are for the private use of the registered guests in each of the four cabins. Phone for rates and reservations.

STATES EAST

This map was designed to be used with a standard highway map.

MAP SYMBOLS

● Non-commercial mineral water pool

■ Commercial (fee) mineral water pool

□ Gas-heated tap or well water pool

〜 Paved Highway

--- Unpaved road

⋯ Hiking road

901 SAND SPRINGS POOL
Sand Springs Road   413 458-5205
■ Williamstown, MA 01267

An historic seasonal plunge located in the heart of the Berkshire Hills in northwestern Massachusetts. Elevation 900 feet. Open May-September.

Natural mineral water flows out of a spring at 74° and is piped to several pools where it is gas-heated and treated with chlorine. The whirlpool is maintained at a temperature of 102°. The swimming pool and toddler's pool are maintained at approximately 80°. A grass beach for lounging is a pleasant addition. Bathing suits are required.

Facilities include changing rooms, sundeck, exercise room, sauna, snack bar, dance floor, picnic tables, and large lawn. A motel, service station, restaurant and other services are available within 10 blocks. No credit cards are accepted.

Directions: From the Williamstown municipal building on US 7, drive north to Sand Springs Rd. Turn right and follow signs to pool.

Sand Springs Pool: This would be the perfect place for a retreat from the heat during a New England summer.

902 The Spa
414 Mohawk Trail   413 774-2951
❏ Greenfield, MA 01301   800-THESPA-1

Beautiful, modern spa with outdoor redwood deck offering a three-state view, located at the gateway to the Berkshires.

Sunken tubs in two indoor private rooms offer individual showers, adjustable air and water jets, and variable lighting, and can accommodate up to six people. The one outdoor tub offers a breathtaking vies. The tubs are maintained at 102° and chlorine treated. Handicap access is available with help.

Massage, a Turkish steambath, tanning rooms, and a sauna are available on the premises along with a juice bar, lounging nooks and games. Special "pampering" packages are available as are private party rentals. Major credit cards are accepted. Phone for rates, reservations and directions.

903 East Heaven Tub Co.
33 West St.   413 586-6843
❏ Northampton, MA 01060

Beautiful, Japanese-motif rental facility located across from Smith College in the Connecticut Valley.

Private-space hot pools using gas-heated tap water treated with bromine are for rent to the public. There are four indoor tubs in private rooms and three outdoor tubs in private, roofless enclosures on the roof. All are maintained at a temperature of 104°.

Sales of saunas, hot tubs and spas are conducted on the premises. Credit cards are accepted. Phone for rates, reservations and directions.

THE SPRINGS OF SARATOGA

The Saratoga Springs area has a two-century-old tradition of providing natural beauty, health giving geothermal water, and the gaiety of its summer race-track season. More than a dozen springs discharge naturally carbonated mineral water along the Saratoga Fault, which is located in a low basin between Lake George and Albany.

In 1909 the state of New York created a Reservation Commission and acquired the land around Geyser Creek, which has now been designated as Saratoga Spa State Park. Some geo-thermal activities are still accessible for public viewing, such as the only spouting geyser east of the Mississippi River.

Bathing in mineral water is available only at the Lincoln and Roosevelt mineral baths in the Park and at the Crystal Spa bathhouse in the city of Saratoga Springs. All baths have separate men's and women's sections using one-person tubs that are drained and filled after each use so that no chemical treatment of the water is necessary.

904A   LINCOLN MINERAL BATHS
518 583-2880
■   **Saratoga Springs, NY 12866**

Traditional mineral bath facility with nearby hotel and conference center operated by Amfac Parks and Resorts. Open all year.

Mineral water flows out of a spring at 53° and is piped to individual tubs in private rooms. Along the way it is heated to approximately body temperature.

No appointment is necessary for a mineral bath. Massage and other spa treatments are available by appointment. All major credit cards are accepted.

Phone for rates, reservations and directions.

904B   CRYSTAL SPA
92 S. Broadway   518 584-2556
■   **Saratoga Springs, NY 12866**

Newly constructed, privately owned spa associated with the Grand Union Motel where the mineral water is available for drinking as well as for bathing. Open all year.

Mineral water flows out of a spring at 52° and is piped to individual soaking tubs where it is mixed with 149° tap water as needed to obtain the desired soaking temperature. Separate facilities are provided for men and women.

New building additions offer expanded services. Sauna, massage, facials, manicures, and pedicures are available on the premises. Pampering packages are available. No credit cards are accepted. Phone for rates, reservations, and directions.

Courtesy of The Crystal Spa

The Crystal Spa: This genuine Victorian gazebo and costuming is reminiscent of ladies and gents coming to "take the waters" during the racing season.

904C   ROOSEVELT MINERAL BATHS AND SPA

■   **Saratoga Springs, NY 12866**

Closed for renovation. No date set for reopening.

Courtesy of The Saratoga Spa State Park

905 BERKELEY SPRINGS STATE PARK
304 258-2711
■ **Berkeley Springs, WV 25411**

Large, traditional bathhouse operated as a state park, located in a narrow valley in West Virginia's eastern panhandle. Elevation 620 feet. Open 361 days per year; reservations recommended.

Two thousand gallons-per-minute of mineral water flow out of several springs at a temperature of 74°. A portion of this water is steam-heated to 102° and piped to five private, one-person bathtubs in the main bathhouse and to thirteen private tiled baths in the Old Roman Bath House. All are drained and refilled after each use so that no chemical treatment of the water is necessary. The Old Roman Bath House is open all year. Mineral spring water is also piped directly to the outdoor swimming pool, which is treated with chlorine and is open from Memorial Day through Labor Day. Attendants are on duty to assist disabled guests. Bathing suits required in public areas.

Facilities include steam cabinets. Massage, heat treatments, and other health services are available on the premises. Visa and Mastercard are accepted. All other services are available in the adjoining town of Berkeley Springs. Phone for rates, reservations, and directions.

Courtesy of Berkeley Springs State Park

George Washington was sixteen when he first visited these springs. Later he purchased property here so that he could enjoy the waters on a regular basis.

I wonder what our founding fathers would have to say about the coed soaks at the Old Roman Bath House?

906   THE GREENBRIER

800 624-6070
304 536-1110

■ **White Sulphur Springs, WV 24986**

A large, historic, health-oriented mineral spring resort occupying 6,500 acres in an upland valley of the Allegheny Mountains, near the Virginia border. Elevation 2,900 feet. Open all year.

Natural mineral water flows out of a sulphur spring at 58° and is piped to individual soaking tubs in separate men's and women's sections of the the Spa and Mineral Baths, where it is heated by electricity to the desired temperature. Tubs are drained and filled after each use, so no chemical treatment is needed. Water from a fresh-water spring is piped to an outdoor pool and the Grand Indoor Pool, where it is treated with chlorine and heated by steam to a temperature of 75°. A hydraulic chair lift is available for the indoor pool. Bathing suits are required.

Facilities include rooms and luxury suites, dining rooms and restaurants, a complete convention center, shops, service station, tennis courts, three golf courses, aerobics studio, exercise equipment, spa and spa salon, and a complete diagnostic clinic. Services include fitness evaluations, daily exercise classes, massage, herbal wrap, facials, manicures, pedicures and full hair services. The diagnostic clinic and shops are available to the public. All other facilities are for the use of registered guests only. All major credit cards are accepted. Phone or write for rates, reservations, and directions.

The Greenbrier, offers the ultimate in luxurious accommodations and facilities.

Courtesy of The Greenbrier,
Dan Day, Photographer

The Homestead: The flow of water at the source spring is so great that several pools can be maintained on a flow-through basis at this 15,000 acre up-scale resort.

907 THE HOMESTEAD
PO Box 2000   800 838-1766
■ Hot Springs, VA 24445

A very large, very historic, luxurious resort on the west slope of the Allegheny Mountains near the West Virginia Border. Elevation 2,500 feet. Open all year.

The odorless mineral water used at the Homestead Spa flows from several springs at temperatures ranging from 102-106°. It is piped to individual, one-person bath-tubs in separate men's and women's bathhouses, where it is mixed to provide an ideal temperature of 104°. Tubs are drained and refilled after each use so that no chemical treatment of the water is necessary. Mineral water from the same springs is used in an indoor swimming pool maintained at 84° and an outdoor swimming pool maintained at 72°. Both pools receive a minimum of chlorine treatment. Use of the spa and all pools is restricted to registered guests only. Bathing suits are required except as indicated in the bathhouses.

Five miles away but still within the 15,000-acre Homestead property are the Warm Springs, which flow at 96°. The rate of discharge is so great that the two large Warms Springs pools, in separate men's and women's buildings, maintain a temperature of 96° on a flow-through basis, requiring no chemical treatment of the water. These Warm Springs pools are open only during the warm months and are open to the public. Bathing suits are optional.

The facilities include over 500 bedrooms and parlors, restaurants, shops, conference center, bowling alley, movie theater, and tennis courts. Recreational activities available on the premises include golf, archery, fishing, hiking, riding, skeet and trap shooting, and tennis, plus skiing and ice skating in the winter. There are many resort services available, some of which are included in the basic room rate. Phone or write for complete information. Visa, MasterCard, and American Express are accepted.

908   HOT SPRINGS RESORT
■   **600 Hot Springs Rd.   828 622-7676**
Hot Springs, NC 28743

Picturesque pools and campground on the banks of the French Broad River in the Great Smokey Mountains. The Appalachian Trail runs between the camp sites and the pools. Elevation 2,000 feet. Open all year.

Natural mineral water flows out of a spring at 100° and is piped to eight secluded, outdoor soaking pools scattered through a wooded area along the river. Pools are cleaned, drained and refilled after each use, so no chemical treatment is required. Four of the pools are equipped with a plastic bubble for winter use. One pool is handicap accessible. Bathing suits are officially required, but some of the pools are very secluded.

Facilities include 150 camping sites ranging from fifty primitive, shaded sites along the river, fifty with water and electric, and fifty full RV hookups. Group sites can be arranged. There are nine camping cabins and one log cottage with a private mineral water soaking tub. A camping supply and grocery store and a snack bar is on the premises. Massage is also available. All other services are one-quarter of a mile away in the town. Call for status of extensive expansions. Visa and MasterCard are accepted.

Phone for rates, reservations, and directions.

Hot Springs Resort takes very good care of its clientele, providing plastic bubbles over four of their pools to keep out the rain, and lattice work around the creekside tubs to provide privacy while soaking.

Photos by Rachel Margolin

909   THE ARMOUR HOTEL
321 E. Main St.   615 699-2180
■ **Red Boiling Springs, TN 37150**

Originally built in 1924, this hotel now operates as a bed and breakfast with old-fashioned country atmosphere and a small bathhouse offering private soaks. Open all year.

Mineral water is heated to a comfortable temperature in the two private bathtubs in a separate bathhouse. A one hour treatment consisting of a soak, steam, and rub down is offered.

The twenty beautifully decorated rooms all have private baths and air conditioning. A restaurant is on the premises serving family style meals and all other services are right in the town of Red Boiling Springs. Space is also available for weddings, parties, and reunions.

Phone for rates, reservations, and directions.

910   RESORT AND SPA AT
WARM MINERAL SPRINGS
San Servando Ave.   813 426-9581
■ **Warm Mineral Springs, FL 34287**

Modern spa, health studio, and nearby apartment complex with a nine-million-gallons-per-day mineral spring, located halfway between Fort Meyers and Sarasota. Elevation 10 feet. Open all year.

Mineral water flows out of the ground at 87° and into a two-acre private lake. It is also piped to a health studio. The lake, which is used for swimming, does not need chlorination because of the volume of flow-through mineral water. The indoor soaking tubs and whirlpool baths are filled with 87° water. The tubs are drained and refilled after each use so that no chemical treatment is needed. Wheelchair access. Bathing suits are required except in private rooms.

Facilities include sauna, gift shop, bakery and snack bar, massage, and hot packs are available on the premises. Apartment rentals are nearby. No credit cards accepted. Phone for rates, reservations, and directions.

Safety Harbor. Workshops and meals to improve your health and beautify you inside and out are offered in luxurious surroundings. More than twenty nutritional, fitness and wellness classes are offered on a daily basis.

911   SAFETY HARBOR RESORT AND SPA
■   105 N. Bayshore Dr.   800 237-0155
    Safety Harbor, FL 34695

An upscale, historic spa, specializing in fitness, beauty and wellness programs, located at the west end of Tampa Bay. Elevation 10 feet. Open all year.

Natural mineral water flows from four springs at approximately 55° and is piped to several pools and to separate men's and women's bathhouses. Gas is used to heat the water. The six individual soaking tubs in the men's and women's bathhouses are drained and filled after each use so that no chemical treatment of the water is necessary. All other pools are treated with a reverse osmosis procedure requiring very little chlorine treatment. The courtyard swimming pool, the lap pool, the indoor exercise pool and the women's plunge pool are maintained at 85°. Two coed hydrojet pools are maintained at 99° and 101°. Bathing suits not required in bathhouses.

The natural mineral water is also used in most of the guest rooms, both restaurants, and in the cooling system.

Facilities feature a 50,000-foot spa and fitness facility, with men's and women's locker rooms, showers, sauna, steam room, weight training room, cardio room, two aerobic gyms, and thirty-five treatment rooms. More than sixty spa and salon treatments and twenty-five supervised exercise classes are offered daily. The Phil Green Tennis Academy offers nine courts, while the Quinzi Gold Academy features a practice range, pro shop and individual instruction. The resort also has two restaurants and a lounge. All facilities and services are reserved for the use of registered guests only. Visa, MasterCard, American Express, and Diner Club, are accepted.

Phone for rates, reservations, and directions.

Courtesy of Safety Harbor

912   COTTONWOOD HOT SPRINGS SPA AND MOTEL

600 Hot Springs Rd.   **205 691-4101**
800 526-SPAS

■   **Cottonwood, AL 36320**

A full range of health services is offered by this destination motel and spa located on nine hundred acres with full recreational facilities.

Two outdoor, hot mineral water swimming pools and eight indoor, private, mineral water tubs are fed by hot salt mineral water piped above ground from a drilling depth of almost one mile. The temperature in the swimming pool is 112°, and the temperature in the private pools is kept at 90°.

Motel rooms and suites, RV hook-ups, a restaurant, conference center, lake, fishing, paddle boats, bicycle and nature walks, picnic area, a golf driving range, massage, and health food store and gift shop are all available on the premises. It is also possible to book family reunions and retreats. Major credit cards are accepted.

Phone for rates, reservations, and directions.

Courtesy of Cottonwood Hot Springs

The hot mineral water to fill this pool comes from 4,800 feet under the earth.

Hernando De Soto may or may not have been the first European on the scene, but today's Hot Springs National Park and the surrounding community have their roots in the 1803 Louisiana Purchase. In 1832, Congress took the unprecedented step of establishing public ownership by setting aside four sections of land as a reservation. Unfortunately, no one adequately identified the exact boundaries of this reservation, so the mid-19th century was filled with conflicting claims and counterclaims to the springs and surrounding land.

By 1870, a system evolved that reserved the springs for the Federal Government and sold the developed land to the persons who had settled it. At the same time, the government agreed to collect the 143-degree geothermal spring water into a central distribution system that carried it to private property establishments where baths were offered to the public. By 1877, all primitive soaking "pits" along Hot Springs Creek were eliminated when the creek was confined to a concrete channel, roofed over, and then paved to create what is now Central Avenue.

In 1921, The Federal Reservation became Hot Springs National Park, custodian of all the springs and the exclusive contractual supplier of hot mineral water to those elaborate establishments that had become the famous Bathhouse Row. It is also the authority that approves every establishment's rates, equipment, personnel and services related to that water.

In 1949, the Park Service installed air-cooled radiators and tap-water cooled heat exchangers to supply a new central "cool" mineral water reservoir. Now all thermal water customers receive their supply through two pipes, "hot" at 143° and "'cool" at 90°.

During the last four decades, declining patronage forced the closure of many of those historic temples built for "taking the waters." However, the last several years has seen a large resurgence of interest in thermal soaking both for therapy and for pure relaxation, so many of the historic Bathhouse Row locations are being refurbished.

For additional information contact the Hot Springs Chamber of Commerce, PO Box 1500, Hot Springs, AR 71902.

913A   BUCKSTAFF BATHS
■   501 Central Ave.   501 623-2308
Hot Springs, AR 71901

One of the historic Bathhouse Row establishments in continuous operation since 1912, located at the south end of the Row near the Visitor Center. Open all year

Separate men's and women's sections offer one-person soaking tubs that are individually temperature-controlled. They are drained and refilled after each use so no chemical treatment of the water is needed. Along with the bath you also get a sitz bath, hot packs, the use of a vapor/steam cabinet, and a needle shower massage. Whirlpool baths and body massage are available.

Facilities include a third-floor coed lounge with separate men's and women's sun decks at each end. Credit cards are accepted.

Courtesy of Hot Springs National Park

In response to the increased interest in stress reduction this family is enjoying a relaxing time together. *Libbey Memorial* is one of the only concessioners actually located in Hot Springs National Park.

**913B LIBBEY MEMORIAL PHYSICAL
MEDICINE CENTER   501 321-1997
AND HOT SPRINGS HEALTH SPA**

■

MEDICINE CENTER

Downstairs, a modern, "Medicare-approved, federally regulated" therapy facility and, upstairs, a modern spa with coed soaking tubs, located on Reserve Avenue, three blocks east of Central Avenue. Open all year.

The Libbey Memorial coed thermal whirlpool (105°) and coed exercise pool (98°) are drained and refilled each day, so no chemical treatment of the water is necessary. Facilities include steam and vapor cabinets and electric hoists at therapy pools. Hot packs, massage, and prescribed treatments such as Paraffin Immersion, Ultra Sound Therapy, and Electric Stimulation are also available. Credit cards accepted.

HOT SPRINGS HEALTH SPA
**501 Spring St.   501 321-9664
Hot Springs, AR 71901**

The health spa's eight large coed soaking tubs are individually temperature-controlled as desired between 102° and 108°. All are drained and filled each day so that no chemical treatment of the water is necessary. Children are welcome. Massage, steam and vapor cabinets, and exercise equipment are available. Credit cards accepted.

Courtesy of Hot Springs National Park

Catering to therapy needs downstairs and recreational fun upstairs, *Libbey Memorial* appeals to the total hot mineral water marketplace.

Courtesy of Arlington Resort

Water from these springs has been keeping people warm since 1875, when the original Arlington Hotel was opened. The present Arlington Resort opened with a gala New Year's Eve party in 1924. The famous President Teddy Roosevelt and the infamous gangster Al Capone have both stayed here.

913C ARLINGTON RESORT HOTEL & SPA   800 643-1502
■   In Arkansas   501 623-7771

A magnificent, luxurious resort in a dominant location overlooking the downtown historic district and Bathhouse Row in Hot Springs National Park.

The in-hotel bathhouse with separate men's and women's sections is open to hotel guests and the public. Private soaking tubs for your mineral water whirlpool bath are individually temperature-controlled and drained after each use so that no chemical treatment of the water is necessary. Massage, hot packs, saunas, sitz-baths, steam baths, and needle showers are available.

A mineral-water redwood hot tub, two tap water swimming pools treated with chlorine, and a multi-level sundeck are reserved for registered guests. The hot tub is maintained at 104°, and the twin pools are maintained at 86° year round.

Facilities include three restaurants and two lounges, beauty and facial salon, exercise room, ballroom, conference and exhibit centers, and shopping mall. Visa, MasterCard, American Express, and Discover are accepted.

913D DOWNTOWNER HOTEL & SPA   800 251-1962
■   501 624-5521

A modern hotel with a large second-floor bathhouse, located on Central Avenue, one block north of Bathhouse Row.

A bathhouse with separate men's and women's sections is open to the public. One-person soaking tubs are individually temperature-controlled and drained after each use so that no chemical treatment of the water is necessary. Whirlpool baths, vapor treatments, hot packs, sitz baths, and massage are available.

An outdoor swimming pool and a hot tub are filled with chlorine-treated tap water, and are reserved for the use of registered guests.

Facilities include a beauty salon, sun decks and two restaurants. Visa, MasterCard, American Express and Discover are accepted.

913E HOT SPRINGS HILTON

800 HILTONS

■ **In Arkansas 501 623-6600**

Large, modern resort hotel located next to the Hot Springs Convention Center, two blocks south of Bathhouse Row.

A bathhouse with separate men's and women's sections is open to the public. One-person soaking tubs are individually temperature-controlled and drained after each use so that no chemical treatment of the water is necessary. Massage is available.

An indoor whirlpool (108°) and an indoor-outdoor swimming pool filled with chlorine-treated tap water are reserved for the use of registered guests.

Facilities include restaurants, lounge, meeting rooms and banquet facilities. Visa, MasterCard, American Express, Diners Club, and Discover are accepted.

Courtesy of Majestic Resort

Courtesy of Hot Springs Hilton

913F MAJESTIC RESORT/SPA

800 643-1504

■ **In Arkansas 501 623-5511**

A unique combination of hotel, motel, and health spa facilities located at the north end of Central Avenue.

A bathhouse with separate men's and women's sections is open to the public. Individual soaking tubs for your mineral water whirlpool baths are temperature-controlled and drained after each use so that no chemical treatment of the water is necessary. Massage is available.

An outdoor swimming pool filled with chlorine-treated tap water and heated in the winter is reserved for the use of registered guests.

Facilities include deluxe rooms and suites, beauty salon, two restaurants and a lounge, old fashioned soda fountain, gift and clothing shops, and conference and banquet rooms. Visa, MasterCard, American Express, and Discover are accepted.

The health spa exterior has been totally renovated to reflect its original art deco theme when it was built in 1936. The lobby still has the original marble floors and columns. The building also serves as the city hall.

914A HALL OF WATERS SPA AND WATERBAR

201 E. Broadway   816 630-0753

■ **Excelsior Springs, MO 64024**

Originally housing a variety of health-oriented activities and the world's longest mineral water drinking bar, this "Haven of Health" has been completely renovated and is now operated by a private corporation. Elevation 900 feet. Open all year; spa reservations required.

Cold (54°) natural mineral water is pumped from wells (which used to be flowing springs) and is piped to the spa where it is gas-heated and used in individual, private-space tubs. After each use, tubs are drained and refilled so that no chemical treatment of the water is necessary. The bathhouse is coed. The indoor swimming pool, using gas-heated, chlorine-treated tap water, is maintained at approximately 75° and open only in the summer. Handicap accessible. Bathing suits are required in this coed pool.

Facilities include dressing rooms, spa services offering steam and light vapor baths, Scotch needle douche, mud baths, salt glow, body shampoos, toning treatments, raindrop therapy, aromatherpay, and professional therapeutic massage.

The water bar serves as the local Visitors Information Center and headquarters for festivals and special events. Completely restored, you may again sample the original Iron Manganese and Calcium mineral waters that made Excelsior Springs famous. The calcium water is also bottled and sold. The bar sells bottled mineral and flavored waters from around the world. All other services are available close by or in the town. Major credit cards are accepted. Phone for rates, reservations, and directions.

914B THE ELMS RESORT HOTEL
Regent and Elms Blvd.   816 630-5500
401 Regent St.   800 843-3567
■ **Excelsior Springs, MO 64024**

A completely restored historic resort, with an emphasis on wellness programs, on sixteen wooded acres, one-half hour northeast of Kansas City. Elevation 900 feet. Open all year.

Cold (54°) natural mineral water is pumped from wells on the property and piped to single soaking tubs in separate men's and women's sections. Customers control tub water temperature by adding hot tap water to the cold mineral water as desired. The tubs are drained and filled after each use so no chemical treatment of the water is necessary.

Chlorine-treated tap water is used in all other pools. The indoor European swimming track is maintained at 75°, the one outdoor hot tub pools are maintained at 100°, and the outdoor swimming pool is solar heated. Bathing suits are required in these public-area coed pools. The Spa is open to the public on a limited basis, as well as to registered guests.

The 10,000-foot spa include cosmetology, hair salon, facials, aloe treatments, herbal wraps, two Swiss and two Vichy showers (in conjunction with other treatments), mineral water and mud bath and massage. Classes are offered in yoga and meditation. Other facilities include individually configured rooms, suites, two restaurants, a cafe (spa cuisine), and tennis courts (under construction). A golf course is available. Bicycles are for rent to travel the naturally wooded areas at the resort. A group challenge-course is on the premises. Major credit cards are accepted. Phone for rates, reservations, and directions.

915 THE ORIGINAL SPRINGS HOTEL AND BATH HOUSE
618 243-5458
■ **Okawville, IL 62271**

An authentic turn-of-the-century mineral spring resort hotel, located in a small town on I-64, forty-one miles east of St. Louis. Elevation 600 feet. Open all year.

Natural mineral water flows out of a spring at approximately 50° and is piped to separate men's and women's bathhouses, where it is gas-heated as needed in one-person soaking tubs. Tubs are drained and filled after each use so no chemical treatment of the water is necessary. The indoor/outdoor swimming pool uses gas-heated tap water treated with chlorine, and is maintained at 85°. Bathing suits are not required in bathhouses. Day use customers are welcome.

Facilities include guest rooms and a restaurant. Massage is available on the premises. Visa, MasterCard, Discover and American Express are accepted. It is less than four blocks to a service station, store and other services.

Phone for rates, reservations, and directions.

---

916 Clearwater Hot Tubs
1201 Butterfield Rd.   630 852-7676
❏ **Downers Grove, IL 60515**

An upscale rent-a-tub facility located in a suburban town twenty-five miles west of Chicago.

Three different types of suits are available. The spa suite included a tub, shower, dressing area, mood lighting, and music. The VIP suite offers a teak tub, shower over the tub for cool-down, cedar sauna and loft area, mood lighting and music. The party suite's tub has special massage jets and includes the shower, sauna, loft area, a full bath, TV and stereo, mood lighting, and a small fridge with complementary water. Pool temperatures are maintained at approximately 100° in the summer and 104° in the winter. Clothing is optional in the private spaces and required elsewhere.

Massage with steam room is available by appointment. Visa, MasterCard, American Express, and Discover Card are accepted. Phone for rates, reservations, and directions.

917 FRENCH LICK SPRINGS RESORT
812 936-9300

■ **French Lick, IN 47432**

The "largest most complete resort in the Midwest," located on 2,600 wooded acres in southwest Indiana, two hours from Indianapolis. Elevation 600 feet. Open all year.

Natural mineral water flows from a spring at 50° and is piped to separate men's and women's bathhouses where it is heated by gas-generated steam, as needed, for one-person soaking tubs. Tubs are drained and filled after each use so no chemical treatment of the water is necessary. All other pools use steam-heated tap water treated with chlorine. The outdoor and indoor whirlpools are maintained at 104°, the dome pool ranges from 72° in the summer to 82° in the winter, and the Olympic swimming pool, for summer use only, is not heated. Bathing suits are required except in bathhouses.

Facilities include two eighteen-hole golf courses, indoor and outdoor tennis courts, equestrian stables and riding trails, guest rooms, nine restaurants and lounges, bowling alleys, conference center, exercise facility, and beauty salon. Massage, body treatments, saunas, steambaths, reflexology, salt rubs, facials, and manicures are available on the premises. Visa, MasterCard, and American Express are accepted. It is three blocks to a service station, store, and other services.

Phone for rates, reservations, and directions.

918   All Is Well Day Spa
506 W. Will Rogers Blvd.   918 341-4771

❏   Claremore, OK 74017

A totally up-to-date spa located in the downtown district of Claremore. Opening in 1999.

Several types of relaxing whirlpool baths are available, each individual mixed. Innovative treatments include Ozone Infrared Saunas and the SomAcoustic Relaxation System, a comfortable reclining chair that soothes the body and mind with 3-D sound and a gentle, circular, wave-like motion. Take an Aroma Bath, a one-hundred percent natural session that uses gentle, sauna-like dry heat to open the pores, allowing microscopic droplets of essential oils to be absorbed into the bloodstream. Tubs are drained, cleaned, and refilled after every use so no chemicals are added to the water.

Also experience the Universal Portal, where your mind and body are immersed in light, color, and relaxing sound, and the Trinity Table, providing a relaxing circular motion that many have referred to as pure bliss. For total relaxation, there is the Hydrosonic Massage. Through the use of water and ultra-low frequency sound, it massages at a very deep level, and you get to keep your clothes on. Also available, for both men and women, are traditional massages and natural facials. Additionally, several natural body wraps are offered. Many other services and products are available for your enjoyment. Location: less than a block off historic Route 66 in downtown Claremore, Oklahoma. From Tulsa, take I-44 north to Catoosa. Take Route 66 north to Will Rogers Blvd. in Claremore. Turn right and it will be on the left side of the street. From Joplin, Missouri, take I-44 south to the Claremore exit. Turn left on SR-20. At Route 66, turn north and go 1 block to Will Rogers Blvd. Turn right and it will be on the left side of the street.

Other attractions in the Claremore area include the Will Rogers Memorial, the J.M. Davis Gun Museum, Will Rogers Downs Race Track, along with numerous lakes and outdoor activities. In fact, All Is Well Day Spa is located in the middle of one of the best antique shopping districts in the state of Oklahoma.

919 EVANS PLUNGE

1145 North River   **605 745-5165**

■   **Hot Springs, SD 57747**

The world's largest natural warm water indoor swimming pool and water park, located at the north edge of the town of Hot Springs in southwestern South Dakota. Elevation 3,800 feet. Open all year.

Five thousand gallons per minute of 87° water rises out of the pebble bottom of the plunge, providing a complete change of water 16 times daily, so only a minimum of chlorine is necessary. Waterslides, traveling rings, fun tubes, and kiddie pools are available at the plunge. Two hydrojet spas (100-104°), sauna, steam room, and fitness equipment are located in the health club. No credit cards are accepted.

A gift shop is available on the premises. All other services are available within one-half mile.

Courtesy of Evans Plunge

Evans Plunge: Less than 60 miles from Mt. Rushmore the kids can find a place to play and the adults a place to relax and soak, all in natural mineral water.

920 SPRINGS BATH HOUSE
501 N. River St.   **605 745-4424**
■ **Hot Springs, SD 57747**

Spa services in an old Victorian sandstone building in historic downtown Hot Springs across the street from the eighty-seven degree river which runs through the town. Elevation 3,580. Open all year.

Hot mineral baths and aroma therapy baths are offered in private soaking tubs (suits not required). The natural mineral water is enhanced with a mineral-rich bath salts to add to your relaxation. Cool baths, saline or hot and warm baths are also offered.

Massage therapy, reflexology, a steam cabinet, facials, salt glo and hydrotherapy are offered. A gift store offering locally-made bath products is on the premises. Camping and RV hookups are within five miles, and gas stations, restaurants, motels, etc. are withing walking distance. Major credit cards accepted.

Wind Cave National Park is twelve minutes away and Custer State Park and Mt. Rushmore, only an hour away. Evans Plunge and the Mammoth Site are within minutes of town.

921 SPRINGS BATH HOUSE AND HOT MINERAL POOL
142 N. Garden St.   **605 745-4424**
■ **Hot Springs, SD 57747**

Large outdoor pool boasting of the natural warm mineral waters Hot Springs is famous for. Located in the center of Hot Springs Old Town, surrounded by the city park. Elevation 3,580. Opening in June, 1999 (call for status).

Natural mineral water from an underground spring at temperatures ranging from 90-100° will be pumped to a large soaking pool that will accommodate between thirty-five to fifty soakers. (No children will be allowed without a doctor's recommendation for therapy.) Bathing suits required.

All spa services will be offered at the Springs Bath House.

GOING NATURAL—PLACES TO STAY

To help those of you who like to stay in places that cater to the naturist lifestyle, included is a list of clubs offering varying types of accommodations. Always call first to check on availability and amenities, and club rules.

CANADA

Alberta

Helios Nudist Association
PO Box 8, Site 1, RR2
Tofield, AB T0B 4J0
403 662-2886

Sunny Chinooks Association
PO Box 33030, 3919 Richmond Road, SW
Calgary, AB T3E 7E2
403 274-8166

British Columbia

Sunny Trails Club
43955 Lougheed Hwy, Box 18
Lake Errock, BC V0M 1N0
604 826-3419

Vancouver Sunbathing Assoc.
10185 164th St.
Surrey, BC V4N 2K4

Van Tan Club
PO Box 423, Stn. A
Vancouver, BC V6C 2N2
604 980-2400

Saskatchewan

Green Haven Sun Club
PO Box 3374
Regina, SK S4P 3H1
306 699-2515

UNITED STATES

Washington

Fraternity Snoqulamie
PO Box 748
Issaquah, WA 98027
425 392-NUDE

Kaniksu Ranch
4295 N. Deer Lake Rd. #5
Loon Lake, WA 99148
509 233-8202

Lake Associates
2174 Hwy. 9
Mt. Vernon, WA 98274
360 424-6833

Lake Bronson Club
PO Box 1135
Sultan, WA 98294
360 793-0286

Oregon

Restful Haven
PO Box 248
North Plains, OR 97133
503 647-2449

Squaw Mountain Ranch
PO Box 4452
Portland, OR 97208
503 630-6136

The Willamettans
3700 Parsons Creek Rd.
Springfield, OR 97478
541 933-2809

Idaho

BareBackers
PO Box 5781
Boise, ID 83705
208 322-6853

East of the Rockies

Gymno-Vita Park
PO Box 121
Vandiver, AL 35176
205 672-7105

Caliente Resort
6500 Land O'Lakes Blvd.
Land O'Lakes, FL 34639
813 996-3700

Club Paradise
PO Box 750
Land O'Lakes, FL 34639
800 237-2226

Cypress Cove
4425 Pleasant Hill Rd.
Kissimmee, FL 34746
407 933-5870

Gulf Coast Resort
13220 Houston Ave.
Hudson, FL 34667-6101
813 868-1061

The Island Group
22146 Dupree Dr.
Land O'Lakes, FL 34639

Lake Como Club
20500 Cot Rd.
Lutz, FL 33549

Riviera Naturist Resort
PO Box 2233
Pace, FL 32572
850 994-3665

Seminole Health Club
3800 SW 142nd Ave.
Davie, FL 33330
954 473-0231

Sunburst Resort
2375 Horn Rd.
Milton, FL 32570
904 675-6807

Sunny Sands Resort
502 Central Blvd.
Pierson, FL 32180-2323
904 749-2233

Sunsport Gardens
14125 North Rd.
Loxahatchee, FL 33470
561 793-0423

Blue Lake club
PO Box 13
Erie, IL 61250
309 659-9297

Fern Hills Club
7330 S. Rockport Rd.
Bloomington, IN 47403
812 824-4489

Lake O'the Woods Club
PO Box 53
Valparaiso, IN 46384

Sunny Haven
11425 Anderson Rd.
Granger, IN 46530
219 277-5356

Sunshower
3263 Mattie Harris Rd.
Centerville, IN 47330
765 855-2785

Tri-State Country Club
79 Drakes Ridge
Bennington, IN 47011
812 427-3914

Berkshire Vista Resort
312 Kittle Rd.
Hancock, MA 01237
413 738-5154

Sandy Terraces
PO Box 98
Marstons Mills, MA 02648

Forty Acre Club
PO Box 309
Lonedell, MO 63060
314 639-0050

Buckridge
21 S. Tuttle Hill Rd.
Candor, NY 13743
607 659-3868

Empire Haven
RD3, Box 297
Moravia, NY 13118
315 497-0135

Bar-S-Ranch
313 Bar-S-Trail
Reidsville, NC 27320
910 349-2456

Nirvana Sun Resort
65 Harbour Dr.
Tabor City, NC 28463
800 378-7072

Oaklake Trails
PO Box 470564
Tulsa, OK 74147

Sun Meadow
PO Box 521068
Tulsa, OK 74152
918 266-7651

Rock Haven Lodge
462 Rock Haven Rd.
Murfreesboro, TN 37127
615 896-3553

Timberline Lodge Resort
Rt. 10, Box 158, Hwy. 70 North
Crossville, TN 38555

White Tail Park
39033 White Tail Drive
Ivor, VA 23866
800 987-6833

Avalon
PO Box 369
PawPaw, WV 25434
304 947-5600

INDEX

This index is designed to help you locate a listing when you start with the location name. The description of the location will be found on the page number given for that name.

Within the index the abbreviations listed below are used to identify the specific state or geographical area of the location. The number shown after each state listed below is the page number where the **KEY MAP** of that state will be found.

AK=ALASKA / 20
CD=CANADA / 30
EA=STATES EAST / 182
ID=IDAHO / 86
MT=MONTANA / 152
OR=OREGON / 62
WA=WASHINGTON / 52
WY=WYOMING / 166

NUBP=NOT USABLE BY THE PUBLIC

W

Z

HOT Springs & Hot Pools
of the Northwest

ALASKA	CANADA
IDAHO	WYOMING
OREGON	WASHINGTON
MONTANA	

and

STATES EAST OF THE ROCKIES

$18.95 ISBN 1-890880-00-0

HOT Springs & Hot Pools
of the Southwest

CALIFORNIA	UTAH
ARIZONA	COLORADO
NEW MEXICO	NEVADA
TEXAS	BAJA (MEXICO)

$18.95 ISBN 1-890880-01-9

Jayson Loam's **original best-selling regional guides to places where you can go and legally put your body in hot water. Edited and produced by Marjorie Gersh-Young.**

Our easy-to-use format provides a complete description and a specific key map location for every spring listed.

Dozens of maps and hundreds of photos helps you make an informed choice, tells you how to get there, and shows you what to expect when you arrive. GPS coordinates included.

Descriptions of primitive free-flowing hot springs and commercial springs include description of physical surroundings, bathing suit customs, directions, and distances to a campground and other services.

These guides also include drilled hot wells and private gas-heated tap water pools for rent by the hour.

Name		
Street		
City	State	Zip

	Order Quan.	Amount
Hot Springs and Hot Pools of the Northwest $18.95		
Hot Springs and Hot Pools of the Southwest $18.95		
Postage: $3 first book, $2 each additional book		
Canadians: Please send in US dollars **BOOK** Make check to: AQUA THERMAL ACCESS 831 426-2956 **MAIL ORDER** Mail to: 55 Azalea Lane, Santa Cruz, CA 95060		TOTAL

S.S. CALENDARS
PRESENTS

NATURIST CALENDARS

in full color

Nature and Nudes
Gorgeous scenery with bodies as nature intended

Hot Springs in Nature
Pictures of some of the most beautiful wilderness hot springs

Preview calendars at www.webpak.net/~sscals
e-mail: sscals@micron.net

A Dippers' Guide to Hot Springs Throughout the West and Elsewhere

Each issue highlights one or two areas of natural hot springs, complete with great stories and anecdotes.

Also includes updates, information on books and maps, the internet, and bits of this and that.

Edited by Skip Hill

Published Quarterly
Single copy price: US $5.00, plus $1.00 postage
Subscription rate per year: US $20.00

Check the Gazette out at: http://www.hotspringsgazette.com

Send check or money order to:
The Hot Springs Gazette
240 North Jones, Suite 161
Las Vegas, NV 89107

Press Catalog

www.mexicomike.com
e-mail: mexicomike@mexicomike.com
Credit Card Orders: 1-800-321-5605
Mail Orders: Roads Scholar Press,
11424 Killion St. #7, North Hollywood,
CA 91601-2650

Spas & Hot Springs of Mexico
$16.95

A practical guidebook with a wealth of information and heartwarming stories about world-class spas that cost one-half of their American counterpart to simple, wilderness hot springs. Included are places renowned for their healing properties, spiritual retreats, and those places that offer traditional spa services.

More Than a Dozen of Mexico's Hidden Jewels $9.95

Stories for the armchair adventurer about places that are truly unique.

Mexico From the Driver's Seat $8.95

Gives an insight into the character of the Mexican people as well as whet your appetite for dozens of locales, both well-known and off the beaten track.

Live Better South of the Border $16.95

Handbook for living and working in Mexico for people of all ages, persuasions, and interests. Internet addresses and advice on starting a business. More than 40 cities and villages compared.

Mexico and Latin American Travel and Business Report (includes hot springs), 20+pages, quarterly
Yearly rate: $38.95 (print) $25.95 (e-mail).

Name: _____

Address: _____

City: _____

State: _____ Zip: _____

Mail Orders: Roads Scholar Press,
11424 Killion St. #7, North Hollywood,
CA 91601-2650
        All payments must be in US Funds

SUBSCRIPTION TITLE	PRICE	$38.95_____ $25.95___ QUANTITY
Spas & Hot Springs	$16.95	_____
Mexico's Hidden Jewels	9.95	_____
From the Driver's Seat	8.95	_____
Live Better	16.95	_____

TX residents add tax: 8.25%   _____
Shipping: $4.00-1, $5.00-2, $6.00 for all _____

TOTAL _____

If you discover something at a hot springs that needs to be revised,
or you come across additional information that you would like to pass along,
write phone, fax or e-mail it to:
Aqua Thermal Access
55 Azalea Lane
Santa Cruz, CA 95060
phone and fax: 831 426-2956
e-mail: hsprings@ix.netcom.com

May You Soak in Peace

Trail Creek Hot Springs, Idaho
Photo by Phil Wilcox

A GOURMET'S GUIDE TO
MUSHROOM COOKERY
WITH SELECTED RECIPES
FROM MASTER CHEFS

EDITED BY MARJORIE YOUNG AND VINCE VIVERITO

Seasonal Feasts
announces publication of a unique
mushroom cookbook
designed for creative cooks

Crab Stuffed Morels

Grilled Thai Sea Bass with
Portobello Compote

Almond Candy Cap Cookies

Hot or Cold Tree Fungus Salad

Bisque of Chanterelles

Blewitt Bread

Wild Mushroom Flan

Smoked Shiitakes

and many more

"These recipes are a cut above the usual, basic recipes...gustatory jewels! I felt as though the chefs were in my kitchen providing me with a private gourmet cooking class." Arleen Bessette, author <u>Taming the Wild Mushroom</u>

"Now and then there comes along a mushroom cook book that is substantially filled with innovative recipes that feature unusual ethnic ingredients.....These are the recipes such as you see featured on the menu of some highly recommended, expensive, 'worth a trip out of your way' restaurant. This is such a cookbook. This is a great little cookbook for someone who really wants to get out and play in the kitchen." Harley Barnhardt, review from <u>Mushroom, the Journal</u>, Fall, 1998

Aqua Thermal Access is expanding its forays into total decadence and enjoyment. We have established an imprint called Seasonal Feasts which will publish cookbooks. Our first offering, From *Duff to Dinner*, includes fungal recipes that are just a bit unusual and with some interesting ingredients. I can't think of anything better than to go out and hunt wild mushrooms in the morning, soak in the afternoon, and in the evening prepare a wonderful dinner with the fresh mushrooms. And, maybe soak again. Please join us.

From Duff To Dinner

$12.95 PER BOOK
plus $3.00 postage and handling for the first book, $2.00 for each additional book

Name_____

Street Address_____

City_____

State_____Zip_____

Number of books _____at $12.95 per book

Amount_____

Postage and handling   Amount_____

Total_____

SEASONAL FEASTS
55 Azalea Lane, Santa Cruz, CA 95060
Phone 831 426-2956   Fax 831 426-2956
e-mail: hsprings@ix.netcom.com